Modern American Lyric

Modern
American Lyric

*Lowell, Berryman,
Creeley, and Plath*

Arthur Oberg

Rutgers University Press
New Brunswick, New Jersey

Publication of this book was partially supported by a grant from the American Council of Learned Societies to the Rutgers University Press in recognition of its contribution to humanistic scholarship. The funds were provided by the Andrew W. Mellon Foundation and are to be applied to the publication of first and second books by scholars in the humanities.

Library of Congress Cataloging in Publication Data

Oberg, Arthur, 1938-
  Modern American lyric.

  Bibliography: p.
  1. American poetry—20th century—History and criticism.
  I. Title.
PS323.5.023   811'.5'409   77-3302
ISBN 0-8135-0826-6

Permission to quote from the following is gratefully acknowledged:

"Poem," from *Departures* by Donald Justice. Copyright © 1969, 1970, 1971, 1972, 1973 by Donald Justice. All rights reserved. Permission to reprint granted by Atheneum Publishers.
Selections from *Pieces* (copyright © 1969 Robert Creeley), *Words* (copyright © 1962, 1963, 1964, 1967 Robert Creeley), *For Love* (copyright © 1962 Robert Creeley), *The Island* (copyright © 1963 Robert Creeley), *The Gold Diggers* (copyright © 1965 Robert Creeley), and *A Day Book* (copyright © 1972 Robert Creeley) all by Robert Creeley are reprinted by permission of Charles Scribner's Sons and Calder and Boyars Ltd., London.
The first line of "Howl," from *Howl & Other Poems* by Allen Ginsberg. Copyright © 1956, 1959 by Allen Ginsberg. Reprinted by permission of City Lights Books.
A selection from *His Idea* by Robert Creeley. Reprinted by permission of the poet.
Selections reprinted with the permission of Farrar, Straus & Giroux, Inc. and Faber and Faber Limited, London, from the following works by John Berryman: *Berryman's Sonnets*, Copyright © 1952, 1967 by John Berryman; *The Dream Songs*, Copyright © 1959, 1962, 1963, 1964, 1965, 1966, 1967, 1968, 1969 by John Berryman; *Delusions, Etc.*, Copyright © 1969, 1971 by John Berryman, copyright © 1972 by the Estate of John Berryman; *Homage to Mistress Bradstreet*, Copyright © 1956 by John Berryman; *Love & Fame*, Copyright © 1970 by John Berryman; *Recovery*, Foreword copyright © 1973 by Saul Bellow; and *Short Poems*, Copyright 1948 by John Berryman, Copyright © 1958, 1964 by John Berryman, copyright renewed 1976 by Kate Berryman. From the following works by Robert Lowell: *The Dolphin*, Copyright © 1973 by Robert Lowell; *For Lizzie and Harriet*, Copyright © 1967, 1968, 1969, 1970, 1973 by Robert Lowell; *For the Union Dead*, Copyright © 1956, 1960, 1961, 1962, 1963, 1964 by Robert Lowell; *History*, Copyright © 1967, 1968, 1969, 1970, 1973 by Robert Lowell; *Life Studies*, Copyright © 1956, 1959 by Robert Lowell; *Near the Ocean*, Copyright © 1963, 1965, 1966, 1967 by Robert Lowell; *Notebook, 1967–68*, Copyright © 1967, 1968, 1969 by Robert Lowell; and *Notebook*, Revised and Expanded Edition, Copyright © 1967, 1968, 1969, 1970 by Robert Lowell.

Barbara

Contents

Preface

One thing critics not themselves writers of poetry occasionally forget is that poetry is composed by actual
human beings, and tracts of it are very closely about them.
When Shakespeare wrote "Two loves I have," reader,
he was not kidding.

—John Berryman

This book looks at the lyric poetry of Robert Lowell, John
Berryman, Robert Creeley, and Sylvia Plath. It does so in
an age when the lyric may be our most significant type of
poetry and literature. It is not unusual to hear of the lyrical
novel, the lyrical drama, and lyrical criticism. Yet this is
not an historical study of the lyric as genre, although it
addresses this matter on enough occasions throughout the
book. To talk about the lyric is to talk about the short or
compressed poem, the poem likely to express the thoughts
and feelings of some "I," the song, the love poem. But already
there are complications. Short poems can, as lyric sequences, build toward long poems. Personas utilizing the
first person may not be private or personal in the least. Song
may be just a way of talking about a short poem never
set or meant to be set to music. And a love poem which
began or seemed to be a love poem need not be a love poem
at all.

The titles of the four chapters of this book reveal a good
deal — Robert Lowell: "*Lowell* Had Been Misspelled LOVEL."
John Berryman: "The Horror of Unlove." Robert Creeley:

"Locate *I/Love You.*" Sylvia Plath: "Love, Love, My Season." Two things strike me as worth commenting on here.
The titles indicate an awareness of a connection or lack
of connection between language and love; the book pursues
this in part, but never as a technical linguistic study or from
the approach of a Structuralist or Phenomenological meth-
odology. Second, the titles suggest a thesis. In some ways,
this is the case; but if so, I would remark how obsessed
with the possibility or impossibility of love so much of
modern literature is, regardless of genre. Yet these chapters
and this book still are readings or, even better *a* reading,
as in some very basic sense all critical books must be.

The four poets I include here continue or continued to
re-examine what their styles and strategies would be. In
turn, some of the critics who have written on them at times
have changed their interpretations of and approaches to the
same writer or his work. A. Alvarez's recent reconsideration,
in his review of Berryman's *Delusions, Etc.,* of extremist
writing and Robert Lowell's admission of an underevalua-
tion of Berryman's *The Dream Songs* are important instances that come to mind. In my own case, I began writing
first on Sylvia Plath. My approach is a reaction against what
the Plath legend or cult — or what the use of Plath to talk
about our Age and Angst — unfortunately has done to an
understanding of her verse. My response and my recording
of that response are formal ones. What joins the four
chapters and what moves beyond the differences of formal
and orphic voice are a concern of mine which I would call
appreciative, corrective, and humanist. If I was led and
helped to evolve a way of talking about these poets in the
way I do, I would have to admit debts to critics as different
as Randall Jarrell and Lionel Trilling, as much as to these
four poets themselves. Lowell, Berryman, Creeley, and
Plath, all share considerable critical intelligences, however
much criticism at times has been forced to disparage one
poet's mind at the expense of another: whether Lowell or
Berryman is a genius; whether Lowell or Berryman has the
more interesting mind; whether Plath is a "miniature mad
talent" or a major minor artist; whether Creeley has little

or no mind at all. These are the kinds of petty, cruel, outrageous questions which modern criticism occasionally has chosen to raise. But even the poets themselves are not free of such lapses. Berryman's nasty poem "In & Out" in *Love & Fame,* which damns Creeley and Lowell's inability to see the achievements of poets as different as Roethke and Creeley are not isolated examples of such behavior. Yet it was the same Berryman and Lowell who drew our attentions to writers who otherwise would have suffered terrible neglect or even gone unnoticed. More than once I have wondered what each of these four poets would think of being in the company of the others in this book. That I consider each of them to have written substantial, moving, and important poetry I hope is never in doubt, even when I address the kinds of failures I see in or threatening their various verse.

Berryman's dislike of Eliot's theory of the impersonality of the poet strikes me as unfortunate because of its short-changing of Eliot and of the complexity of Eliot's theory. But it may in the end have been important for Berryman to make that point, however much it proved a disservice to Eliot. Never has it been more necessary to acknowledge in the works of so many modern writers a personalism so extreme that we may conclude by wishing that the works had written themselves, that the despair and pathos recorded had no man or woman behind them.

Introduction

Nothing is a substitute for anything else.

The arrival of the new poetry or the new lyric has been announced often enough. With the particular densities and intensities of Robert Lowell, John Berryman, Robert Creeley, and Sylvia Plath, we are in the presence of the shaping of a lyric in which the poet seems to be playing and working out his life and death on paper, fighting some dream out to its relentless end. Lowell worries over whether we think we are getting the real Robert Lowell; Berryman, whether overneed can be met and transformed into great art; Creeley, whether enough is ever enough; Plath, whether she can manage so much suffering and atrocity. We learn not only that nothing is a substitute for anything else but that it is in our loving and dying that we are most ourselves.

What happens as each poet seeks to establish love and to bring his particular love poem into being, the following four chapters will trace; and the concluding epilogue will examine the implications of that search. What kind of reader this new lyric desires and demands we shall see each poet addressing both as a formal and personal concern.

Though these poets devote their major energies to the writing of variant versions of the new lyric and though my major attentions in each chapter look at that situation and development, the issue is more complex. I also see these poets writing out of an older, humanist tradition which has

1

not given up on lyric or love, at least in a very important part of their lives and works. Not only Berryman but Lowell and Creeley and Plath intend their poems to terrify and comfort, in the service of love.

So the new lyric of these poets, however much it may differ over preferences for perfection of the life or of the work, in the end is more likely to want *both*, like Malamud's Fidelman, even when the likelihood seems less and less available to the life and the art.

The lyric of Robert Lowell is not that of Robert Creeley. The lyric of John Berryman is not that of Sylvia Plath. The different forms which that new lyric takes or fails to take, whether willfully or helplessly, whether out of confusion and delusion, or out of vision and craft, the arguments of my four chapters directly and indirectly seek out. What these poets share is what their lyric is not. It is not the "Poem" of Donald Justice:

> This poem is not addressed to you.
> You may come into it briefly,
> But no one will find you here, no one.
> You will have changed before the poem will.
>
> Even while you sit there, unmovable,
> You have begun to vanish. And it does not matter.
> The poem will go on without you.
> It has the spurious glamor of certain voids.
>
> It is not sad, really, only empty.
> Once perhaps it was sad, no one knows why.
> It prefers to remember nothing.
> Nostalgias were peeled from it long ago.
>
> Your type of beauty has no place here.
> Night is the sky over this poem.
> It is too black for stars.
> And do not look for any illumination.
>
> You neither can nor should understand what it means.

Listen, it comes without guitar,
Neither in rags nor any purple fashion.
And there is nothing in it to comfort you.

Close your eyes, yawn. It will be over soon.
You will forget the poem, but not before
It has forgotten you. And it does not matter.
It has been most beautiful in its erasures.

O bleached mirrors! Oceans of the drowned!
Nor does it matter what you think.
These are not my words now.
This poem is not addressed to you.[1]

It is not "The New Poem" of Charles Wright:

It will not resemble the sea.
It will not have dirt on its thick hands.
It will not be part of the weather.

It will not reveal its name.
It will not have dreams you can count on.
It will not be photogenic.

It will not attend our sorrow.
It will not console our children.
It will not be able to help us.[2]

To be fair to Donald Justice and Charles Wright, they
themselves write poems counter to this new lyric as often
as they find some terrible, deadly attraction to the cancellation and absence it offers. If the lyric of Lowell, Berryman,
Creeley, and Plath is anything, it is insistent on addressing,
and on addressing the intimate "you" in us, what may be
resistant to the very things it holds out for our regard and

---

1. Donald Justice, "Poem," *Departures* (New York: Atheneum Publishers, 1973), p. 38.
2. Charles Wright, "The New Poem," *Hard Freight* (Middletown,
Conn.: Wesleyan University Press, 1971-73), p. 19.

care. It is still insistent, if afraid of being photogenic or of offering easy dreams, in consoling and helping in weathers which might seem most inhospitable to love. Looking back to an older lyric which may no longer be possible, these four poets nonetheless spend much of their energy in resisting the kind of new lyric here which Justice and Wright so ironically and seriously hold up to transparent light. In that process, another new lyric appraises its own possibilities, if in the very act of having them questioned and even, sometimes, sadly denied.

Chapter One

Robert Lowell: "*Lowell* Had Been Misspelled LOVEL"

Daddy, they're all footmarks
　　　　　—Harriet Lowell to her father, on *Notebook*

The evening of June 6, 1971, at the Mermaid Theatre in London, Robert Lowell read from his poetry. He read only from *Notebook* (1970), and seven poems in all — four loving poems for his daughter Harriet, a poem for Robert Frost, a poem ostensibly about a go-go dancer but really about "western marriage," and a bad but revealing poem about an older, rejected woman poet who accused Lowell of having no human concern for unestablished writers. But before reading his own poems, Lowell read poems of other important moderns: Randall Jarrell, Allen Tate, Elizabeth Bishop, Ezra Pound. He also talked before and in between his readings. The things which occupied him were various, but what never varied was the passionate care expended in talking about them. He talked about Wallace Stevens's last poems and about their particular music as it is shaped by that poet's sense of aging and mortality. He talked about Frost as perhaps the only sane man in a mad, tragic family. By the time the audience's questions were over, Lowell had rejected a request to read beyond the two hours he had

already been reading and talking. And he had to endure,
under the guise of a question, abuse from a young man
about how unwitty, unimportant, and overrated a poet he
was. By that time, Lowell's anecdote, told earlier in the
evening, about his daughter and the poems of *Notebook*
— "Daddy, they're all footmarks" — took on an even more
complicated context than Lowell could have intended in
telling it in the first place.

I begin with the personal and the anecdotal. Not because
Lowell himself so often relies upon these as major strategies
in his poems from *Life Studies* (1959) and the books which
follow, but because that evening at the Mermaid brought
together for me some of the major problems and pleasures
that attended Lowell and his poetry then and that attend
him, perhaps even more, now:

The difficulties of the public and private art and life. The
unending need for and demanding weight of a tradition and
homage to poets alive and dead. The awareness of the poet
aging, and, so, "moved into position to die." The reputation
which a poet may gain or suffer or have change, once or
more in a lifetime. The need for love and fame, and the
nagging doubt not only of whether they will arrive but of
whether they can be joined. The question of whether love
and marriage ever were meant to go together at all. The
problems of writing the long poem. Explicitly, and by
dolphin-like implication, these were the matters which sur-
faced that evening. To these and to some related matters,
I wish to turn in the course of this chapter.

> *A genius temperament should be handled with care*
>   —Robert Lowell

Robert Lowell has been writing for over thirty years, and
he has been conscious of development, reputation, and the
nonlinear way the poet proceeds in the world. T. S. Eliot,
upon seeing as a young man some of the cave drawings
in France, understood how art never improves. For as
important a poet as Eliot or Lowell, to talk of progress in
the arts or in one's own art is impossible, if not unhelpful

and misleading.

The matter of reputations has dogged Lowell with each successive book; and with his excursions into other genres and literature, into new styles and old styles brought complexly back, Lowell has continued to be the one English-speaking and -writing poet whom critics and poet-critics in particular have seen as *the* poet or, vehemently, not the poet of the last ten or fifteen years.

The poetry which Lowell wrote and published before *Life Studies* recorded an able, sometimes precocious poet in search of materials for an art as well as a style to manage that art. If Lowell later rejected much of what he felt this earlier work represented to him as art and in a life, he also has gone back to parts of it in successive volumes, reworking some of the poems, including others in new contexts, and showing the same respect for craft and language and intelligence which marked his work from the very beginning. And some of the earlier poems from *Land of Unlikeness* (1944), *Lord Weary's Castle* (1946), and *The Mills of the Kavanaughs* (1951), have settled into familiar anthology pieces which to those critics who have disliked Lowell's later departures are representative Lowell.

But to determine what is representative in a poet's work proves problematic both for the writer and the critic. The poet learns that others may mistake what he wants to do or to depart from. If he lives long enough, Lowell may be forced to endure changes in his status as a major or major minor poet. In one of the poems from *History* (1973), Lowell writes, with both passion and distance:

> Kokoschka at eighty, saying, "If you last,
> you'll see your reputation die three times,
> or even three cultures; young girls are always here."[1]

1. Robert Lowell, "1930's 3," *History* (New York: Farrar, Straus and Giroux, 1973), p. 107. Hereafter, references to poems in this volume *(H)* will be included in the text. The criticism of Lowell included in this poem is that of Donald Hall. Lowell's quoting is very close to Hall's actual words and phrasing in "The State of Poetry — A Symposium," *The Review*, Nos. 29-30 (1972), 40.

Lowell knows only too well that this may be his fate and history. In another, later poem from *History*, Lowell records with both passion and distance:

> Ah the swift vanishing of my older
> generation — the deaths, suicide, madness
> of Roethke, Berryman, Jarrell and Lowell,
> "the last the most discouraging of all
> surviving to dissipate *Lord Weary's Castle*
> and nine subsequent useful poems
> in the seedy grandiloquence of *Notebook*."
>
> (*H*, 204)

As an updated *Howl*, this passage takes its swipe at unfavorable criticism while reaching out to assume the savage indignation of the mad, unmad talents of Allen Ginsberg and Jonathan Swift. It is not sheer reportage or quotation, any more than it would have been in the anecdotal context of any poem from *Life Studies*. It is clear that Lowell does not agree with this adverse judgment upon his development or descent as a poet. But he places this disagreement in the larger context of those other, kindred-spirit poets and, by implication, in the context of the critical reception which greeted each new work by them in their lifetimes or after. Where Lowell separates himself from them is in the fact that he remains alive; his work, nonposthumous; himself, not just Robert Lowell, but *a* Lowell, whom the critic at times has thought it his right to address even more demandingly — a Lowell of Boston "where the Lowells talk to the Cabots/And the Cabots talk only to God."

> *"Is not style," as Synge once said to me, "born out of the shock of new material?"*
> —W. B. Yeats, *Autobiography*

Robert Lowell has the kind of sensibility which made Norman Mailer interested in creating a portrait of him in *The Armies of the Night*, tellingly subtitled *History as a Novel, the Novel as History;* and Mailer has the kind of sensibility which so intrigued Lowell that he made an artful life study of Mailer in one of his *Notebook* poems. Mailer's sense of Lowell as a man and poet who wishes and needs to be loved by anyone vaguely his peer, and after the measure of gossip and rivalry has been granted, supports my own reading of the man and the work which I shall pursue later in this chapter. But, at this point, I would like to look at a section of *The Armies of the Night* in which Mailer is concerned with finding some extended metaphor for *himself*:

> Now Mailer was often brusque himself, famous for that, but the architecture of his personality bore resemblance to some provincial cathedral which warring orders of the church might have designed separately over several centuries, the particular cathedral falling into the hands of one architect, then his enemy. (Mailer had not been married four times for nothing.)[2]

Mailer's third-person-first-person writing, his Christian and martial and marital metaphor, and his overriding, extended metaphor of himself as cathedral are exact and telling. (And ironic, because Mailer is a Jew.) I would not want to think of Lowell in the same terms. But in the tense complexity and even contradiction of the architecture, Mailer and Lowell approach one another.

Beyond the egos which both men continually confront their readers with, there exist two interesting, interested men. They have and are not just personalities, but sensibilities. If this has always been more outrageously the case with Mailer, since *Life Studies* Lowell increasingly has depended upon that fact.

To talk about Lowell is immediately to address contradiction. He can be medieval in his obsession with last things, Renaissance in his admiration for the infinitely gifted man, classical or Augustan in his judgment and taste, romantic

2. Norman Mailer, *The Armies of the Night* (New York: The New American Library, 1968), p. 17.

and Victorian and modern by turn. And it may be in his position as modern that he tries to hold together what in any other age either never would have had to be reconciled or would have been so overwhelming as to lead to madness or death. Since Yeats, we have not had a poet who has taken such extensive stock of who he is, where he is, and what he takes poetry to be.

Stock-taking in modern poetry is something which we find natural and which we have even come to expect. What distinguishes this activity in Yeats and Lowell, however, is that it proves to be a dramatic, thematic center. In part, it is the stock-taking of all major art, whether that of Shakespeare in *The Tempest* or of Joyce in *A Portrait of the Artist as a Young Man;* but whereas the modern critic is in danger of overreading or even misreading Shakespeare in such terms, with Joyce, Yeats, and Lowell he is on safer ground. These moderns so insistently go over the ground on which their art is to stand that it becomes a major part of that ground itself.

The form which Lowell's stock-taking discovers is close to the "agonizing reappraisal" which separates Lowell in "Memories of West Street and Lepke" both from the lobotomized, hence unthinking, Louis Lepke, "*Murder Incorporated's* Czar," and from John Foster Dulles, who originated the phrase.[3] Lowell's violence is likely to be verbal rather than physical, just as his policy of brinkmanship is likely to be some level of irony within a poem rather than within international policy and politics. But such strategies exist only for establishing or confirming a human context. At worst, Lowell's stock-taking can reduce him to writing about Lowell reading Lowell or about reading critics reading Lowell and writing on Lowell. On such occasions, we are not very far from Beckett's Krapp listening to Krapp listening to Krapp, or from Portnoy on himself.

At best, stock-taking involves Lowell in focusing upon

3. Robert Lowell, *Life Studies* (New York: Farrar, Straus and Cudahy, 1959), p. 86. Hereafter, references to poems in this volume *(LS)* will be included in the text.

the ways in which the public and private man so steadily inform and contradict one another. For Lowell, this proves part of that search for style which takes the poet into considerations of where and how style can turn into stylization, or stylelessness. *Life Studies* remains a seminal book because in it the poet is concerned with "*ton*," "ambiance," "eclat," "decor," "air," "atmosphere." This book shows Lowell distinguishing between false styles and true styles, styles that concealed and styles that defined. Later work of his extends this concern, and in the *Notebook* poems — which include those from *Notebook 1967-68* (1969), *Notebook* (revised and expanded edition, 1970), *History* (1973), *For Lizzie and Harriet,* (1973), and *The Dolphin* (1973) — Lowell at times turns to consider the history of style, playfully and devastatingly creating labels as hybrid as "wrecked gingerbread Gothic" and "suburbia – proletarian."

The background against which Lowell in *Life Studies* takes stock, addresses questions of style, and reveals or hides from us his sensibility, frequently is that of his parents and grandparents. It is a world in this century and the nineteenth, and it shares much of the eighteenth-century concern with decorum. It is a world of men and a society of women, although Lowell, like Henry James in his novels, like Eliot in "The Love Song of J. Alfred Prufrock," and like Pound in *Hugh Selwyn Mauberley,* is aware of the ways in which these depart from and reverse that distinction, both as improvement and as deterioration. A society of men and a world of women, after all, would create its own losses and problems. What has happened to feeling and thought in these worlds and societies — since they are plural in complexity and fact — determines much of what we take Robert Lowell to be.

The *Life Studies* prose section, "91 Revere Street," shows how problematic feeling has become, and it details a situation which the rest of the book bears out. Lowell writes of his father in "91 Revere Street":

He was deep — not with profundity, but with the dumb

depth of one who trusted in statistics and was dubious
of personal experience.

(*LS,* 17)

And, in partly echoic words, of his mother:

She did not have the self-assurance for wide human experience; she needed to feel liked, admired, surrounded by
the approved and familiar.

(*LS,* 32)

As different as Lowell's parents are, they share, in his portraits of them in "91 Revere Street," problems in feeling.
They risk feeling too little or too much. Lowell, in turn,
both as child and as adult, saves himself from emotional
exhaustion through wit which exposes discrepancies and
insists upon saving discriminations. Yet no one more than
Lowell is aware that distinction-making is not an inevitable
good; to his mind, the Christian Scientist whose special language and religion insist that "asthma" is simply " 'growing-
pains' " (*LS,* 41) comes in for as much criticism in "91 Revere
Street" as the social, racial upper-Bostonian shock at the
naval officers' talk of " 'grade-A' " and " 'grade-B wops' "
(*LS*,16). These Brahmins are shocked more by the language
than the division and are perhaps more guilty than the naval
officers on that account. But there are other distinctions
which exist and which are available to Lowell as poet and
man — what it meant to be a boy, rather than a girl, at
Brimmer; what it meant for a school to have *ton;* what it
meant at home to be a boy rather than a man; what it meant
to be a "cit" rather than a professional, navy man. The
words and the distinctions they carry continually resonate
in "91 Revere Street" for Lowell: *"boy," "ton," "life," "career," "cit."* They explode in the manner that words explod-
ed for Stephen Dedalus and Joyce: "belt," "suck," "hot,"
"cold," "kiss," *"Tower of Ivory,"* "Dolan." The release of
such words, for Joyce and for Lowell, is epiphanic, painful
and discomforting with the discoveries each word brings.
   In miniature and on its own large scale, "91 Revere Street"

shows Lowell endlessly distinguishing, complicating irony by irony. Behind the piece are the most overarching ironies of all: this house is the house which Lowell's father as naval officer was not supposed to have; and, since Lowell's father has to be away from it so much of the time, it explains metaphorically, if not literally, "why Young Bob is an only child" (*LS*, 46). The ironies of "91 Revere Street" touch every other section of *Life Studies* and prove typical of the books which followed.

Lowell's ironies succeed in conveying the impression that we are in the presence of a man and poet concerned with remaking the language and taking on nothing less than the whole literary and intellectual establishment, even modernism itself, matching wits with Sir James Frazer and Carl Jung, Sigmund Freud and Joyce, Friedrich Neitzsche and William Empson; letting ambiguity and ambivalence (notable in his young daughter's "sky-blue corduroy" in "Home After Three Months Away," *LS*, 83) come as close to one another and to the poet and reader as they are ever likely to do; committing and mocking every critical fallacy ever formulated; acknowledging the moderns and the classical moderns, modern literature, and the classics. In two lines of "Fall 1961" from *For the Union Dead* — "Nature holds up a mirror. / One swallow makes a summer"[4] — Lowell tilts with Cervantes and John Heywood, M. H. Abrams and Aristotle. And it is typical of the man.

In the case of Lowell and Freud, there is the continuing suspicion that Lowell wishes to have it both ways. He is both beyond Freud and not beyond Freud. If he complains in his poem, "Eloise and Abelard" (*H*, 55), that Eloise cannot be understood by means of orthodox analysis, he does not dismiss the possibility that she, like Abelard and Lowell, can also be understood in psychological terms. The many moments back in *Life Studies* — whose title suggests aesthetic as well as psychological meanings — where he playfully

---

4. Robert Lowell, *For the Union Dead* (New York: Farrar, Straus and Giroux, 1964), p. 12. Hereafter, references to poems in this volume (*FUD*) will be included in the text.

dealt with Freudian motifs were never totally transcended, nor were they meant to be:

> Terrible that old life of decency
> without unseemly intimacy
> or quarrels, when the unemancipated woman
> still had her Freudian papa and maids!
>
> ("During Fever," LS, 80)

> Tamed by Miltown, we lie on Mother's bed;
> the rising sun in war paint dyes us red;
> in broad daylight her guilded bed-posts shine,
> abandoned, almost Dionysian.
>
> ("Man and Wife," LS, 87)

> In the mornings I cuddled like a paramour
> in my Grandfather's bed,
> while he scouted about the chattering greenwood stove.
>
> ("Dunbarton," LS, 67)

Each passage shows how emancipated and unemancipated, how aware and yet dependent and helpless Lowell in fact is. And this is so in spite of the devices which he uses and which seek to make him all-seeing, all-knowing, and free.

Lowell does, however, separate himself from the less aware figures who people his poems. He possesses an ability to confront what for lesser sensibilities would be only an impasse. Lowell renders the impasse or dilemma and then attempts to have us see it as an irony which, if it cannot be put aside, can be worried over, approached, and enjoyed. Metaphorically, it is the "portly, uncomfortable boulder" of "Terminal Days at Beverly Farms" (LS, 73), the " 'unhistoric' soul" of Lowell's cemetery father in "Sailing Home from Rapallo" (LS, 78), and the "fishbone" which sticks in the throat of Boston in "For the Union Dead" (FUD, 71). The first image, that of the "portly, uncomfortable boulder," Lowell goes on to individuate in "Terminal Days at Beverly Farms"; the boulder "bulked in the garden's center — /an irregular Japanese touch." By the time the poem ends, this boulder has been associated not just with Lowell's father's "Bourbon 'old fashioned,' " but with the father himself, and by extension, with the craft and person of Robert Lowell. The boulder, which first "bulked," becomes a mark of graceful, subtle beauty, "an irregular Japanese touch." It is one of those telling, perfectly right details which show us the presence of a major poet who painstakingly yet obliquely wishes to be sure that we see and understand his intentions on the smallest and largest scale.

Lowell's concern with being major and with possessing genius runs through the poems particularly in and after *Life Studies,* as if that book was for Lowell the kind of breakthrough which confirmed talent while it showed Lowell coming into and standing on his own. If *History, For Lizzie and Harriet,* and *The Dolphin* at times annoyingly push the question of fame and genius to the foreground, they do so with the same relentlessness with which Lowell's "boulder" is put in our path and shown to be part of Lowell's very particular design or garden.

Lowell's relentless, exacting sense of himself and of his art is evident throughout his work. In "Home After Three Months Away," Lowell asks, "Is Richard now himself again?" (*LS,* 83). Both the histrionic, pathetic Richard II and the loveless, self-locked Richard III are recalled by Lowell and by his readers in order to underline what exists as problems in definition and fulfillment in the poet. These problems go far beyond the limited context of the return from hospitalization for mental difficulties; even in times of health, they are very much in Lowell's thoughts. In one of the recent poems included in *The Dolphin,* Lowell's "*I am, I am, I am*" asserts what it risks denying.[5] And it echoes Sylvia Plath's same words from both her novel *The Bell Jar* and from her poem "Suicide off Egg Rock" from *The*

---

5. Robert Lowell, "The New," *The Dolphin* (New York: Farrar, Straus and Giroux, 1973), p. 65. Hereafter, references to poems in this volume (*D*) will be included in the text.

Colossus.[6] Although Lowell's *"I am, I am, I am"* refers in context to Caroline Blackwood, Lowell's third wife, Lowell's own sense of self is equally if not more at stake. Unlike Sylvia Plath, however, Lowell is intent on establishing loving sanity in the midst of madness and loss, just as he is unable to talk about self except in relation to his life's work or art. If Lowell is more public a poet than Sylvia Plath, this puts even more demands upon him in living and writing about the private details of a life.

A neutral tone is nowadays preferred

— Donald Davie

To speak in a flat voice
Is all that I can do

—James Wright, "Speak"

When Lowell spoke of "the monotony of the sublime," he did so against an American background in which "art is always done with both your hands."[7] In this paradoxical and difficult phrase about the sublime, Lowell seems to be talking less about the art of rising or sinking in poetry, for which he deserves both blame and praise, than about a situation, peculiarly American but also contemporary British, where every artist, minor and major, is in search of a style for an art and a life. Against a background of preferences for a literature of silence or understatement or impersonality which the modern poet at times picks up without even knowing it, there emerges that kind of poem and vision which threatens to end in flatness and uncertainty, but which in the process of getting written always manages to show a fair measure of competence and even excellence.

---

6. Sylvia Plath, *The Bell Jar* (New York: Harper & Row, 1971), pp. 178, 274; Sylvia Plath, "Suicide Off Egg Rock," *The Colossus and Other Poems* (New York: Alfred A. Knopf, 1962), p. 35.

7. Robert Lowell, "The Problems of the Artist," *Under Pressure*, e.d. A. Alvarez (Baltimore: Penguin Books, 1965), pp. 163-64; see also Robert Lowell's "our monotonous sublime" in "Waking Early Sunday Morning," *Near the Ocean* (New York: Farrar, Straus and Giroux, 1967), p. 24. Hereafter, references to poems in this volume *(NO)* will be included in the text.

It becomes what I might call a poetry which parodies paradigm, a paradigm of what we take the modern poem to be — that multileveled poem with its slide-off ending balanced enough to make us debate whether its closure provides us with some felt, thoughtful stance or mere mannerism which seeks to mask its noncommitment. Familiar endings of familiar Lowell poems — "his last words to Mother were: / 'I feel awful,' " ("Terminal Days at Beverly Farms," LS, 74); "Then morning comes, / saying, 'This was a night,' " ("Myopia: a Night," FUD, 33); "a ghost / orbiting forever lost / in our monotonous sublime," ("Waking Early Sunday Morning," NO, 24); "bright sky, bright sky, carbon scarred with ciphers," ("End of a Year," H, 207) — come to stand for what we think of as Lowell and Lowellian to the extent that poets after Lowell have taken over the devices involved, if often without the painstaking procedures by which Lowell developed them.

But more than closure is involved. What Lowell does in ending a poem extends to the entire body of a poem and to the way he brings a book together or decides to publish it. The ways in which Lowell builds his ironies, adjusting things as we have known two other New Englanders, Emily Dickinson and Frost, to do; the ways in which the publication of a single volume or several at the same time (the tripublication of History, For Lizzie and Harriet, and The Dolphin, for example, seeks not just to establish 1973 as Lowell's annus mirabilis, but to affect the way we read every poem and every volume) — all these strategies are very close to what we take Lowell and his poetry to be. And such strategies relate to our task of locating the poet and the poet as man in the poem.

With figures like John Berryman and Robert Lowell, the whole concept of a persona has become so complicated that it has been removed from what was once an essentially literary matter, a means of helping define the modernism of Yeats, Pound, Eliot, Frost, Stevens, and W. C. Williams, to a matter which often challenges the very criteria and terminology of art. Sometimes the line between person and persona is so fine that the two become indistinguishable.

In order to deal with this, the reader must become a connoisseur of the art of gradations.

When Lowell asked in "Waking in the Blue," "What use is my sense of humor?" (LS, 81), he was not, as the critic John Bayley suggested, abandoning irony,[8] but depending upon some ideal reader, ironist *par excellence.* This moment in "Waking in the Blue" is analogous to others in "Skunk Hour" when Lowell announces, through a complexly modern persona, "My mind's not right" or "nobody's here" (LS, 90). His mind is both not right and better than right; nobody's here, and everybody who cares about poetry is here. More problematic, but still related to these instances, is the moment in "Eye and Tooth" when he ventures, "Everyone's tired of my turmoil" (FUD, 19). At worst, Lowell is forestalling or disarming his critics. At best, Lowell hopes that his art will leave us with other assessments of what is nonetheless burdensome and wearing.

I can think of no other modern American poet who spends so much time and energy not only in creating and complicating his ironies, but in being sure that we are aware of his strategies. Here are the concluding stanzas of "The Old Flame":

> Poor ghost, old love, speak
> with your old voice
> of flaming insight
> that kept us awake all night.
> In one bed and apart,
> we heard the plow
> groaning up hill —
> a red light, then a blue,
> as it tossed off the snow
> to the side of the road.

> (FUD, 6)

---

8. John Bayley, "Robert Lowell: The Poetry of Cancellation," *Robert Lowell: A Portrait of the Artist in His Time,* ed. Michael London and Robert Boyers (New York: David Lewis, 1970), p. 191.

Lowell is able to turn an old cliché, "my old flame," into a phrase that will make that cliché take on a new, metaphoric resonance. It proves useful and precise for the kind of nostalgia which the poet wishes to record. In these two concluding stanzas, everything from red stop lights to red-light districts to blue movies and blue jokes crosses the reader's mind. The "groaning" and "the snow" are implicitly, if not explicitly, sexual. But they are sexual in the same ironic light which presents the situation of being "awake all night" not in the context of love or love-making, but of memory of insight which has long since gone and been replaced by insight of another kind. The phrase "one bed and apart" defines the scene as precisely as the poem's title. In the face of the sentimentality which Lowell allows himself in the next to last stanza, the action of the snowplow is important in creating needed distancing. Yet the poem does not have a slide-off "tossed off" ending, however much Lowell wishes us to entertain that bad joke. The ending is not "tossed off" because Lowell has not moved from feeling to undercutting feeling. Instead, he has kept that delicate balance of admitting and controlling feeling throughout. In the last stanza, Lowell is able to call our attention not only to his meanings but to the devices whereby those meanings are achieved.

Over and over, Lowell wants to be sure that we are on to what he goes about and intends. He portrayed his grandfather in his poem, "Grandparents," as "dipping sugar for us both," and seen "to walk there, chalk our cues, / insist on shooting for us both" (LS, 68-69). Lowell's criticism is loving and tender; the overbearing nature of the grandfather disappears in the affection with which he is called back. I can recall being annoyed and even offended by these moments. My quarrel lay with my inability to separate the grandfather's tactics from those of Lowell. I no longer read the poem in that way, but see the very real humor with which Lowell calls attention to the bittersweet meanings and strategies of his verse. There is criticism of the grandfather, surely, on Lowell's part. But the grandfather and Lowell also offer comfort and security and love, in the situation of a life and in the medium of an art. The two realms come together, at the same time that they remain separate for us and for Lowell.

One of the greatest pleasures and frustrations with Lowell and his poetry is that we are never done with them. There is always one more complication, one more edge to get by but never blunt or destroy. Even in an introduction by Lowell to another poet's posthumous book or in a dedication to one of his own, the syntax or the arrangement of the words on the page involves us in more complexity than we first might have thought apparent or possible. Here are a small part of Lowell's introduction to Sylvia Plath's *Ariel* and his full dedication to his own *Notebook 1967-68* (and, later, to *Notebook,* but with the two lines of blank spacing gone):

This poetry and life are not a career; they tell that life, even when disciplined, is simply not worth it.[9]

for HARRIET
Even before you could speak,
without knowing, I loved you;
and for LIZZIE[10]

In the first passage, is it clear whether Lowell thought Sylvia Plath's final work worth her death? In the second passage do not daughter and Lowell's then-wife blend and become one, despite the punctuation? In a way reminiscent of Wallace Stevens's poems, Lowell's poems commonly circle back at their conclusion: to their titles, to their beginnings, and to the complications developed throughout the bodies of the poems.

To think of Lowell and Stevens is revealing in other re-

---

9. Robert Lowell, Foreword to *Ariel* (New York: Harper & Row, 1966), pp. x-xi.
10. Robert Lowell, *Notebook 1967-68* (New York: Farrar, Straus and Giroux, 1969), unnumbered dedication page. Hereafter, references to poems in this volume *(Nbk 67)* will be included in the text.

gards. Stevens's "Thirteen Ways of Looking at a Blackbird" could have gone on *ad infinitum,* at least in one sense, and that is part of the meaning of the poem. So could the men and the metaphors and the bridges (bridges and metaphors and men as the makers-of-bridges and, or as, metaphors) in "Metaphors of a Magnifico." And no one more than Stevens would have been aware of that — "It can never be satisfied, the mind, never."[11] What is in store for the reader of Stevens comes close to what awaits the reader of Lowell. There arises the confrontation of one more image, one more perspective, one more circling, circular irony. Two passages of Stevens particularly come forth when I think of Lowell's verse. The first is one of his *Adagia;* the second, part of a piece which he did on W. C. Williams's work:

Poetry is a response to the daily necessity
of getting the world right.

If a man writes a little every day, as William does, or used to do, it may be that he is merely practicing in order to make perfect. On the other hand, he may be practicing in order to get at his subject . . . Is not Williams in a sense a literary pietist chastening himself, incessantly, along the Passaic?[12]

In both passages, I see a defining modernism which Lowell is heir to. It is not a poetry of cancellation or absence or silence, but a poetry which must make and remake itself, again and over again, in order, like the perpetual lover, to get the world right. Stevens and Williams, however different from one another and from Lowell, prefigure Lowell's unending habit of refining and revising, metaphoric and actual, in order to get things right. And it was in *Life Studies* that Lowell first grappled with where he might stand in relation to some of the major moderns and to the traditional

11. Wallace Stevens, "The Well Dressed Man with a Beard," *The Collected Poems* (New York: Alfred A. Knopf, 1957), p. 247.

12. Wallace Stevens, *Adagia* and "Rubbings of Reality," *Opus Posthumous* (New York: Alfred A. Knopf, 1957), pp. 176, 257-59.

modernism which preceded him and of which he would
become a part.

This is my mother and father I'm talking about — Alexander Portnoy (1933-)
                                               —Philip Roth (1933-)

Can I call the police against my own family?
                                               —Robert Lowell

The exactions of *Life Studies* and the books that followed
did not deny the earlier work of Lowell. But in the baroque,
Marian imagery of *Land of Unlikeness* and *Lord Weary's
Castle,* and in the tortured, loveless relationships presented
in the poems of *The Mills of the Kavanaughs,* Lowell
seemed to be using language and rhetoric as a way of de-
flecting more personal things. R. P. Blackmur's complaint
about *Land of Unlikeness* — "There is not a loving meter
in the book" — pointed to a problem which concerned far
more than prosody and which even *Life Studies* and the
later books are never able to put aside.[13]
What is new about the poems in *Life Studies* is not just
or even primarily the turning to more private materials and
a more flexible language, but the decision of the poet to
examine his thoughts, his emotions, and his art in ways
which had not been made available to him in the earlier
books. There is the sense of leisure on the part of a man
who believes in the value of thinking and feeling, of type
and print, without reducing art to a sedentary trade removed from the world of action and even protest. In one
of the *Notebook* poems, Lowell looks back upon an earlier,
younger self and wife and parodies the leisure they once
wanted more of. He turns that leisure into a kind of death-
in-life:

---

13. R. P. Blackmur, rev. of *Land of Unlikeness, A Collection of Critical
Essays,* ed. Thomas Parkinson, Twentieth-Century Views (Englewood
Cliffs, N. J.: Prentice Hall, 1968), p. 38. Hereafter, this collection will
be noted as *Parkinson.*

Young, tottering on the dizzying brink
Of discretion once, we wanted nothing,
but to be old, do nothing, type and think.

(*Nbk 67*, 4)

Happily, the ironies of the lines make us aware that Lowell
is denying or reversing nothing at all. For the poet of *Life
Studies* was dizzy with indiscretion, wanted everything,
and knew the limitations and dangers of the contemplative,
intellectual, and artistic life.

Life Studies makes explicit by its analytic, psychological
title the kind of book Lowell intended. Poem by poem, section by section — and the endless italics, quotations, and
quotation marks, parenthetical and foreign words and
phrases — make us aware how the effort of the entire book
is to get things right. In "91 Revere Street," as we saw earlier
in part, Lowell worries over the meaning of every sound,
word, and sentence. This is suited to the rite of initiation
which the section records. Yet "91 Revere Street" is not
just about a modern-day Stephen Dedalus. Beyond that, and
more important for the larger body of Lowell's work, it
presents the figure of the poet who must learn what com-
prises style and sensibility and how to distinguish (as
Lowell's relative, the poet Amy Lowell was unable to do)
between "poetry" and "*chinoiserie*" (*LS*, 38). If, in the
course of reading *Life Studies,* we find ourselves judging
some of the weaker poems, in particular "Father's Bed-
room" and "For Sale," as *chinoiserie,* Lowell should understand why, even though he may not agree with us.

A tour de force as precocious as what it mocks, "91 Revere
Street" risks turning into a linguistic comedy and, at times,
tragedy. If this prose section of *Life Studies* is about anything, it concerns how and why Lowell is and what it means
to be, an only, lonely child; although Lowell presents this
in the form of a crude, pathetic joke at the end of "91 Revere
Street," its implications touch everything else in that section
and in the rest of the book. The first 384 of *The Dream*

Songs, Berryman said, are about the death of his father.[14]
Life Studies is about a modern-day Aeneas who must learn
lovingly to carry not just his father on his back but to carry
and carry back the body of his mother as well, as the metaphor in "Sailing Home from Rapallo" indicates.[15] "In the
grandiloquent lettering on Mother's coffin,/*Lowell* had been
misspelled LOVEL" (*LS,* 78). In their lives and deaths,
Lowell's mother and father help him re-examine the possibilities of bridging language and love.

> *No one like one's mother and father ever lived*
> —Robert Lowell

Instead of the literary, loveless marriage and figure of
Anne Kavanaugh which Lowell gave us in *The Mills of the
Kavanaughs, Life Studies* chronicles the bad, loveless marriage of his parents. His father's two coronaries (complicated in one of the *Notebook* poems by his "invisible
coronary" for which Lowell as son is guilty), the family
history of heart trouble, the poem for Hart Crane, which
is probably the best of the poems in the section of homage
poems – all these point to what is central in *Life Studies*
or, as Lowell encourages us to say, what is at heart.

If older members of Lowell's family at times suggest to
Lowell the loving possibilities and options which his
parents never provided, it is his own attempts in *Life Studies* to see and to locate himself as son, husband, father,
and lyrical poet which offer him a way out of the impasse
of being an only child and only a child. That the figures
he singles out for the homage poems all possessed lyrical
gifts relates as much to loving as to literary matters. Only
in the creation of loving relationships could Lowell hope
to satisfy want or what Berryman calls in his dream song
for Theodore Roethke "overneeds."

---

14. William Meredith, "In Loving Memory of the Late Author of *The
Dream Songs,*" *The Virginia Quarterly Review,* 49 (1973), 77.

15. For other important comparisons between Lowell's poetry and the
Aeneid, see Thomas Vogler, "Robert Lowell: Payment Gat He Nane,"
The Iowa Review, 2, No. 3 (1971), 64-95.

For Berryman, "Father" was "the loneliest word in the one language.[16] For Plath, Daddy always waited to haul her in to death. For Lowell, his absentee father causes him to write one of the most curious, three-line poems in the midst of the fourteen-line *Notebook* poems:

To Daddy

I think, though I didn't believe it, you were my airhole, and resigned perhaps from the Navy to be an airhole — that Mother not warn me to put my socks on before my shoes.

(*H*, 116)

Unlike Sylvia Plath's poem, "Daddy," but like the many of Berryman's poems in *The Dream Songs* for his father, Lowell's "To Daddy" is a love poem. Lowell acknowledges the playful, irreverent humor and possibility of his father as "asshole" in the first two lines; but by the time the next and last line has concluded, Lowell's father has become the affectionate subject and object of a poem that is neither inverted nor perverse. It is a real love poem, though a small and minor one. On the other hand, Lowell, like Berryman, is more likely to discover love in his poetry not through a recovered father but through loving friends who happen to be, or to have been when alive, writers. And, almost always, lyrical talents: Ford Madox Ford, George Santayana, Delmore Schwartz, and Hart Crane.

Who asks for me, the Shelley of my age,
must lay his heart out for my bed and board
                                        —Robert Lowell

The poem for Hart Crane in *Life Studies* is more important to the book and to later work of Lowell's than might

---

16. John Berryman, *The Dream Songs* (New York; Farrar; Straus and Giroux, 1969), no. 241, p. 260. Hereafter, references to this volume *(DS)* will be given in the text and by Dream Song number.

at first be apparent. In it Lowell is able to take advantage of but never abuse the ready pun offered to him in Hart Crane's first name. The poem is as much about the possibility of heart or love as about the history and tradition of the lyric. Catullus, Shelley, Walt Whitman, Hart Crane, and Robert Lowell all prominently enter into it. In the figures of Whitman and Crane, Lowell draws our attention to Crane's loveless life and to what Crane shares with the pathetic Whitman, whose voyeuristic looking in old age upon lovers Lowell intended to recall in one of the stanzas in his poem, "Skunk Hour."[17] In one of the later *Notebook* poems, it is also Whitman whom Lowell imagines becoming (as Whitman himself became all men) and rivaling in this long poem, his own variant of *Leaves of Grass.* By the time of the *Notebook* poems, Crane's urban and historical long poem, *The Bridge,* in search of connection, completion, and loving, also is in Lowell's mind.

Lowell moves in his *Life Studies* poem on Crane beyond the situation of Whitman and Crane (note the painful puns in "lay" and "board") and against those who would be *bored* by Crane's story to the only rightful relationship which Lowell as poet and we as readers can assume, the lover who will give what love was denied to Crane in his lifetime. And it is at this juncture that love and fame become explicitly connected. That this poem happens to be written as a sonnet strategically joins it to all those unrhymed and often rhymed sonnets of loving homage and about love and fame which occupy so large a space in the *Notebook* poems.

Lowell sympathizes with and yet rejects the voyeurism and inversion of love in Whitman and Crane. But these things also concerned him in "91 Revere Street." One of the crudest moments in all of Lowell's work precedes the ending of this prose piece, which tells why Lowell is an only child — Billy Harkness, a naval acquaintance of Lowell's father, pretends to be Admiral De Stahl ("the Man") commanding Lowell's father ("Bobby"):

---

17. Robert Lowell, "On 'Skunk Hour,' " *Parkinson,* p. 133.

"Bobby me boy," the Man says, "henceforth I will that
you sleep wifeless. You're to push your beauteous mug
into me boudoir each night at ten-thirty and each morn
at six. And don't mind me laying to alongside the Missus
De Stahl," the old boy squeaks; "we're just two oldsters
as weak as babies."

(LS, 46)

This moment returns to another, earlier in the piece, about
Amy Lowell's migraine headaches caused by listening to
the sounds of honeymooners in the next room (LS, 38).

Both instances concern not just voyeurism, but the reduction of language to something less than communication, specifically communication as a form of love. Like his distant
cousin Amy, Robert Lowell hears his parents' arguments
not as words but as sounds. And he feels "drenched" in
their "passions" (LS, 19). Since, in a very important sense,
his parents lacked loving passions, Lowell is drowned
rather than renewed in them. Language again records something other than love. The major force of Life Studies becomes the struggle to reverse that direction.

Amo ergo sum
–Ezra Pound, "Canto LXXX"

Inasmuch as I am loved I am
—Robert Lowell

The aspiration in Life Studies is to achieve permanence.
Lowell does so with the awareness that no art is beyond
the dangers of neglect, desecration, and change. This is evidenced in the poems and the very title of For the Union
Dead; the sensibility and strategies behind this book,
despite the more formal look of some of the poems, are
close to those of Life Studies. Life Studies, if it did not per-
manently settle problems of style for future poems of the
poet, at least made clear to Lowell how much familial, domestic things, parents, wife, child, and house, would have

to be engaged by him, lengthily and relentlessly, if he were ever to know what Lowell and love could have to do with one another.

The poems in *Life Studies* and *For the Union Dead* seek to establish a loving language. This search is complicated in these books by the fact that Lowell is aging. He moves through his forties and then at and after fifty charts his "passage from lower to upper middle age" (*H*, 152). If Lowell is fortunate enough to have escaped the fate of having a middle income, he is not so fortunate with middle age. Like Berryman, he is "stuck with middle" (*DS*, no. 340).

Lowell returns in his *Notebook* poems and in their long, extended publishing history to what the four carefully arranged sections of *Life Studies* in part aimed at, the writing of the long poem. *Life Studies* reveals Lowell considering himself in early or lower middle age. The *Notebook* poems, extending over several years, reveal Lowell looking at later middle age, steadily and at different points in time.

In some of the translations and plays which Lowell did in between the writing of these long poems — in *Imitations* (1961); in the translations which make up a major part of *Near the Ocean;* and in the plays in *The Old Glory* (1965; revised edition, 1968) — Lowell does not so much disperse his talents as try to find ways to avoid writing tired poems in some monotonous sublime. And, during the span of years after *Life Studies* and before the publication of the *Notebook* poems, Lowell does manage to write one major long poem, "Waking Early Sunday Morning." This poem, like the earlier poems "Beyond the Alps," "Skunk Hour," and "For the Union Dead," moves toward some poetry of statement and monument.

Monuments are marks of love and fame. Yet Lowell's hope in his "Note" to his revisionist *History* that he has "cut the waste marble from the figure" is no new concern of his for a monumental art. The section of homage poems in *Life Studies,* his interest throughout all of his books in dead writers and their lasting works, and his translations, particularly those in which writers confront the graves or fates or reputations of other writers, are typical. What has happened by the time we get to *History* is that the questions of fame and age are more fully upon him. This urgency is shown in the very history of *History* which, after all, cannot be considered by itself but must be read along with, and against, *For Lizzie and Harriet* and *The Dolphin*. History comes out of *Notebook,* which in turn came out of *Notebook 1967-68*. The movement from the dated to the time-conscious to the timelessly memorial is part of Lowell's intention. But it is complicated by his awareness that such easy divisions are impossible and fallacious. As a student of history, Lowell knows how time and the timeless also can be one.

Part of the change in Lowell's involvement with fame can be indicated by comparing the role of Lowell's daughter Harriet in "Growth," one of the *Notebook* poems where she dramatically moves from preteenager to teenager, with that of her in "Home After Three Months Away" (83), one of the *Life Studies* poems.[18] In this poem, Harriet is only a baby or young child. Her father has just returned from spending time in a mental institution. But he is still so unfunctioning that he cannot start anything by himself. Harriet starts him shaving (in the institution he had no razor) by dipping his shaving brush in the toilet bowl. What is entrusted to her is a matter of love. She returns her father to a loving, living community. She gets him going again: shaving, and by implication, writing, talking, moving, and loving. What is entrusted to her in the other and later poem, "Growth," is also love, but love as fame. She is given in this poem words which assure Lowell that she will complete Lowell's long poem upon his death. Beyond the whimsy and the love looms the consuming question of fame. And the continuing *Notebook* poems perpetuate and intensify that concern. Having started his own London fire by moving to England, fathering a new child and marrying a new wife, and leaving Lizzie and Harriet behind, Lowell suggests in

---

18. Robert Lowell, "Growth," *For Lizzie and Harriet* (New York: Farrar, Straus and Giroux, 1973), p. 42. Hereafter, references to poems in this volume (*FLH*) will be included in the text.

the tripublication of three books that 1973 may indeed be
his *annus mirabilis* in literary victories as well. Lowell's
Book of the Year is as important to him as his "*Book of
the Century.*"

Permanence in verse, set against the ravages of time and
death and change, informs the major sonnet sequences written over the centuries, particularly those of the Renaissance.
If Lowell wished to avoid in his *Notebook* poems what he
called "the themes and gigantism of the sonnet" (*Nbk 67*,
160), at the same time he counts upon these for forceful
support.

Sometimes Lowell's wish for the permanence of fame gets
implicated in rivalries with other poets and in an inability
to admit debts or to see how original other poets are. In
the case of Berryman, however, Lowell at least admitted
how much of Berryman's defining, quirky talent in *The
Dream Songs* escaped him when some of these poems first
came out.[19]

Berryman concluded one of his poems from *The Dream
Songs* with the line, "(Frost being still around)" (no. 36).
There was a time when Frost *was* still around. But Frost
now is dead, along with a host of other poets and poet-
critics: Roethke, R. (Richard) P. Blackmur, Schwartz, Sylvia
Plath. And Lowell is left more and more alone, as Berryman
wrote in his dream song no. 153:

> I'm cross with god who has wrecked this generation.
> First he seized Ted, then Richard, Randall, and now
>   Delmore.
> In between he gorged on Sylvia Plath.
> That was a first rate haul. He left alive
> fools I could number like a kitchen knife
> but Lowell he did not touch.

With Berryman's eventual suicide, these lines take on even

19. Robert Lowell, "For John Berryman," *The New York Review of
Books*, 6 April 1972, p. 4. Hereafter, references to this journal will be
given as *NYRB*.

more power. Things narrow to Lowell.

Like Berryman, Lowell makes out of the deaths and suicides of modern and earlier writers one of the most moving,
agonizing centers in his work. What had been a limitedly
literary *ubi sunt* motif in some of Lowell's translations assumes in the *Notebook* poems increasingly private meaning
for him as a poet and as a man.

In giving the revised, enlarged edition of *Notebook* the
title *History,* Lowell intended both private and public significance for that word. "What is history? What you cannot
touch" (*FLH,* 31), he wrote in a poem which first appeared
in *Notebook 1967-68.* This is closer to the way in which
History, as *For Lizzie and Harriet* and *The Dolphin,* proves
historical. Lowell's sense of history, like that of Yeats and
Pound, is lyric and elegiac rather than narrowly philosophical or historical. When Lowell turns to history or to
prehistory, it is biography which interests him. The figures
who attract him from history and literature and legend, who
were also prominent in poems which preceded the *Notebook* sonnets, frequently are pairs of sad, tragic, sometimes
violent lovers: Paolo and Francesca, Lancelot and Guine-
vere, Dante and Beatrice, Eloise and Abelard, Sappho and
Phaon, Romeo and Juliet, Antony and Cleopatra, Orpheus
and Eurydice. In some cases, one of the pair is a poet, the
poet as lover. And the love or loveless lives of modern writers particularly intrigue Lowell.

If Lowell attempted in *Life Studies* to understand more
fully his name and self and the nature of love, his sonnets
continue and complicate those movements. As Lowell
moves through the *Notebook* poems, he has to rediscover
what his and man's nature and lot are. Although the movement is not always consistent, we can observe a changing
attitude toward man. Lowell moves in the sonnets from a
Marxist (man is what he makes) to an Existentialist or
Nihilist-Existentialist (man is what he does) to a lyrical (man
is what he loves) sense of man. *"What you love you are,"*
Lowell writes in one of his recent poems from *The Dolphin*
(48).

How do I love thee? Let me count the ways
                                    —Elizabeth Barrett Browning

But you can't love everyone, your heart won't let you!
                                    —Robert Lowell

The publication of *History, For Lizzie and Harriet,* and
The Dolphin in 1973 addresses a question which concerns
literature as much as it does a loving life. The titles, together
with the fact and occasion of their publication at the same
time not only establish love and fame as central but point
to the strategies which are to be involved. *History,* the largest work of the three, contains, revises upon, and adds to
the poems which first appeared in the two *Notebooks; For
Lizzie and Harriet* is a sequence of poems which Lowell
creates (also from the *Notebooks*) but which he wishes to
keep separate from the *History* poems; and *The Dolphin*
mostly contains new poems which appear in book form for
the first time. Behind this elaborate ordering and reordering
lie the facts of Lowell's life. Since the publication of the
revised *Notebook,* Lowell divorced Elizabeth (Lizzie) Hardwick and had a son by the woman (Caroline Blackwood)
who became his new wife, the dolphin of the one book.
But things are neither so simple nor so separate. Lizzie is
as present, perhaps even more present, in *The Dolphin;*
Caroline cannot be confined to the pages of her book; and
Lowell and his daughter Harriet, whom he had by Lizzie,
keep denying the very structuring which part of Lowell
seems to need for his art and life. In a very basic regard,
nothing at all has changed. For Lowell's seasonal cycle in
the two *Notebooks* was in the end as unhelpful in approaching major meanings as the biblical-through-modern-history
arching which *History* offers. Against the more superficial
orderings and divisions, runs the strain, *"What you love
you are."* When people whom Lowell loves and continues
to love enter upon the scene, if in different and changing
ways, dilemmas are exposed and Lowell's long art is asked
to float the impossible.

Ted Hughes, in his note to the Poetry Book Society's selection of Sylvia Plath's *Ariel,* wrote of those beautiful things she hoarded in her late poems. When I read the continuing venture of Lowell's sonnets, I think of a similar hoarding. There is the impression that Lowell wants to let nothing go, to get it right, poem by poem, in a procedure which I discussed earlier in connection with Lowell's style and sensibility and with modernism. But hoarding can also be dangerous and deadly. In the use of an endlessly expandable sonnet sequence, Lowell may have found a dead end, in a form which, in a somewhat less heart-torn life, might have set him free.

Life by definition breeds on change

—Robert Lowell

Lowell's revised *Notebook,* although it recorded unfaithfulness and affairs, still was a book of love for Harriet and Lizzie. Against the breathlessness of lines elsewhere in the book which recorded the passion of Lowell for some younger woman or girl, a passion which spoke more of lust than of love — "When you left, I thought of you each hour of the day, / each minute of the hour. each second of the minute"[20] — Lowell wrote poems like "Obit," the last and one of the most moving in the book:

In the end it gets us, though the man knew what he'd
    have:
old cars, old money, old undebased pre-Lyndon
silver, no copper rubbing through . . . old wives;
I could live such a too long time with mine.
In the end, every hypochondriac is his own prophet.
Before the final coming to rest, comes the rest
of all transcendence in a mode of being, stopping
all becoming. I'm for and with myself in my otherness,
in the eternal return of earth's fairer children,
the lily, the rose, the sun on dusk and brick,
    the loved, the lover, and their fear of life,

---

20. Robert Lowell, from "Mexico," *Notebook,* revised and expanded edition (New York: Farrar, Straus and Giroux, 1970), p. 104. Hereafter, references to poems in this volume *(Nbk)* will be included in the text.

    their unconquered flux, insensate oneness, their painful
        'it was . . .'
    After loving you so much, can I forget
    you for eternity, and have no other choice?

(Nbk, 261)

Lowell manages here a meditative, dramatic stock-taking
which reaches toward the discovery of elegy and lyric as
one. The last two lines extend and complicate the tensions
which inform the entire poem, while moving from rhetorical
question to some dynamic point of rest. The poem is at
once private and public, and it establishes love at the expense neither of inconsistency nor of closure.

This poem is redone as the concluding poem in *For Lizzie
and Harriet.* Its fourteen lines are essentially unaltered, but
a new line is added. It is printed as the first and separately
from the other lines: "Our love will not come back on for-
tune's wheel —" (*FLH,* 48). This line previously appeared
in another poem in the revised *Notebook* (143), and the strategy is typical of Lowell's revisions. What is more central,
however, concerns what this added line does to the poem
and how it connects with larger problems in the three recently published books.

We know the reason, from Lowell's private life at least,
for the inclusion of the additional line. But whether it
wrecks or meaningfully complicates the earlier version of
the poem proves a less simple matter. Ironically, by the inclusion of this new dimension, Lowell sacrifices an ambiguity in the concluding lines and even the carefully balanced
tensions of the entire sonnet. The line, while connecting
with the imagery of chance and choice which haunts the
Notebook poems, really is part of a poetry of statement at
variance with the rest of the poem. The finality of the earlier
poem derived from everything which challenged it. In the
new version, the finality diminishes the rich, meaningful
ambiguity of the earlier poem.

What I see happening in the new version of "Obit" relates
to problems Lowell has in bringing his *Notebook* poems
into alignment with changes in an ongoing life. To live is

to change; to live is to love; therefore, to love is to change — this is one of the syllogisms operative in the sonnets. Such a syllogism, when joined to Mailer-like games of what constitutes fact, fiction, and reputation, places upon Lowell's art a strain which that art may find impossible to bear. If we were not tired of an earlier Lowell and his turmoil, Lowell may now sound too much like the poet playing out his guilt, and trying to cheer himself up.

> For Christ's sake, don't cry, you idiot! Live or die, but don't poison everything
>
> —Saul Bellow, Herzog

It is easy to be unfair to Lowell, particularly since Lowell has been so magnanimous a poet before. No one knows more than he the nature of the undertaking which he began, part consciously and part unconsciously, in the first *Notebook*. After *Life Studies* and *For the Union Dead,* after work in translation or in genres other than poetry, and after the writing of a string of extended major poems, Lowell began the *Notebook* poems under the burden of more expectations than even he was likely to have wished.

The sensibility of the man behind the earlier poems continues to stand behind and to permeate the new, long poem. The Lowell who, in "91 Revere Street," spoke of his father as "grimly and literally that old cliché, a fish out of water" (*LS,* 18), addresses in the *Notebook* poems the same old questions of cliché and of metaphor and fact. He concludes his revised *Notebook* poem on Pound, " 'To begin with a swelled head and end with swelled feet' " (120). Metaphor becomes fact, along with the fact of Lowell's own prosodic and physical feet. Such a moment is reminiscent of the last lines from the *Life Studies* poem, "Waking in the Blue," "We are all old-timers, / each of us holds a locked razor" (82); or the last lines from "Home After Three Months Away," "I keep no rank nor station. / Cured, I am frizzled, stale and small" (*LS,* 84). What has escalated in the *Notebook* poems is the seriousness with which Lowell playfully continues to hold every word and phrase and idiom up to the light. When he writes in *History*, "Old age is all right, but it has no future" (64), the wit is even graver than it once had been.

The particularly American problem of early or late liter-ary reputations is reshaped in the *Notebook* poems into a volitional speeding up of the vision of laurels after the grave and after fame. If love and fame are part of the major mean-ings of Lowell's sonnets, the emphasis on fame threatens to become disproportionate. In part, Lowell wishes to have it both ways — to have fame both in and after this life, and to keep the love of both Lizzie and Caroline.

Lowell has to believe he has the love of Harriet and of his second and third wives. He has to believe he has glad-dened his own lifetime, the lives of those closest to him, and the lives of his artful readers. He has to believe he has written *the* American long poem with the old, novel plot (one man, two women) and with the prose richness of the lyrical novel, a substitute and remedy for the still unwritten great, long American novel. At least if we read the history of the American novel in that way. But need is not quite fact. Lowell has his dolphin and he is Arion and Apollo. But what he offers, "an eelnet made by man for the eel fighting" (*D*, 78), suggests intricacy and cunning and strength as much as it calls into question whether the net will hold, the big fish stay, the work survive. Lowell is as playful as the dolphin. He is caught, caught up, and tries in the seemingly unending sonnets to have love, in his net of language, catch and catch on.

But however much Lowell, in his particular use of the sonnet in *The Dolphin* and the two other recent books, ref-uses to falsify experience and art, the resultant impression too often is that of self-generating sonnets desperately try-ing to keep and assure love. Lowell's device of using three adjectives, repeated from the poems in *Life Studies* through the *Notebook* poems, may at base be related to quintessen-tially lyric, three-note utterances ("How do I love thee?"; "The moon slides west")[21] but it may also become mere mannerism.[22] Similarly, the sonnet is ideally a form for some quintessential love poem, but it may easily descend to a parody of that form and intention. And this is the unfortunate situation with many of Lowell's *Notebook* poems.

Poems from *Life Studies* and *For the Union Dead* occasionally were so successful in the creation of ironic distances that the poet at times risked being read out of his poems. The danger with Lowell's latest work is that he has to depend upon being there so often and so much. Lowell's attempts at assigning *Notebook* lines and poems to other people, at turning some of them into poems for voices, usually conclude by sounding like more poems by Robert Lowell, except that variety has been replaced by monotony and humorlessness.

Even the revisions are tedious, making most of the poems slightly better, losing some good one-liners in the process, but serving more as deflections of what the poems' intentions and meanings really are. Lowell's habits of revising, from comments of critics-poets-friends and of his own, are legendary. What is objectionable in the poems which lead to *History* and the two other volumes is that too much of the conspicuous waste proves just waste. Whether Flaubert's "mania for phrases dried his heart" (*Nbk,* 38) or "mania for phrases enlarged his heart" (*H,* 104) reveals sheer quibbling. The quibble centers upon which ambiguity, not whether ambiguity, is preferable. What never proves in doubt is how both versions relate to Lowell's own strategy as poet-lover and implicit criticism of that strategy in these poems.

Strange love talk, is it not?
  —George Meredith

---

21. Josephine Miles does not consider Robert Lowell; but for a discussion of the three-note cry of quintessential lyric utterance, see Josephine Miles, "Styles in Lyric," *Style,* 5 (1971), 226-27.

22. Marjorie Perloff does not connect Lowell's use of three adjectives with quintessential lyric. But, for a discussion of the debasement of the device, see Marjorie G. Perloff, *The Poetic Art of Robert Lowell* (Ithaca, N.Y.: Cornell University Press, 1973), pp. 126-27.

References in the notebook poems to Aztec heart-sacrifices dramatically point to Lowell's concern with the metaphoric significance of a family history of heart trouble and of his father's "invisible coronary."

Lowell's *History, For Lizzie and Harriet, and the Dolphin* are most moving and successful when they reveal the poet anatomizing his own and other hearts in the way we have known him to do before. If Lowell understands with Yeats that images break hearts, he understands with Stalin "an unusual lust to break the icon" (*H*, 143). When in *Life Studies* he wrote of Joyce and Freud as "the Masters of Joy" (53), he did so not only ironically but on a nonironic level as well. It is important that these two men were humanists, two essentially poetic, metaphoric minds, breakers and makers of images. By the time of the *Notebook* poems, Lowell has moved toward a position which announces the death of a Symbolist or even post-Symbolist past. "We were kind of religious, we thought in images," Lowell concludes one of the poems gathered most recently in *For Lizzie and Harriet* (46). Behind the nostalgia and the wish still to think and write in loving images, there is a toughness and a reservation about the redeeming value of literature itself. Such toughness and reservation inform all of the work which we take to be Lowell's best.

The real strengths of *History, For Lizzie and Harriet,* and *The Dolphin* consist in the extent to which Lowell is able to continue to lay his heart on the board, to judge the disparities between "*Lowell*" and "LOVEL," to assess whether love can go with marriage or whether the poet has heart (again, the bad jokes or lines of popular songs which are in the background and typical of Lowell), and to determine whether love can go with fame. What has happened in Lowell's life lends resonance and new meanings to some of the poems which first appeared in the earlier *Notebooks*: the poem about Allen Tate and Lowell's daughter, in which she relentlessly notes his age and aging; the poem about Tate's twin sons fathered at sixty-eight; the poem on Frost; the poem on Milton which considered Milton's marital difficulties, his poetry, and his tracts on divorce; the recurrent poems which looked at love and fame and dying in connection with Lowell's own life, those of other writers, and those who would outlive him and perhaps even his large work.

Lowell continues to do enough of his own worrying about and over what constitutes his true or real self. He seems able to write most convincingly when he composes under the pressure of life, of a man who refuses to stop thinking and feeling, and thinking about them both. There are all the unsettleables: Whether art is worth or reflective of the life; whether love is possible; whether he can love at fifty or older; whether he can be loved if he cannot love himself; whether as poet and man he has gladdened the lifetimes and things he touched.

This last unsettleable question motivated his poem on Frost, a poem which first appeared in the *Notebook 67* (74). In the poems included in *For Lizzie and Harriet* and *The Dolphin,* specifically those domestic poems where Lowell is a lyric, elegiac historian and thus writes on his own home grounds whether actually living in America or England, the question of whether Lowell has brought joy to himself and to others is most fully upon him and finally answered contradictorily. Perhaps Lowell does not know or it is too soon for him to know or not for him to tell.

This contradictory sense, when it derives not from uncertainty but from "that grandeur of imperfection" and from an "open ending," insisted upon for a life and an art, connects with an earlier and for me a more representative and definitive Robert Lowell. But I would not stress connection and continuity of sensibility and style at the expense of what is innovative in these three books. If Lowell is original in anything here, it is in his ability to apply what he did in books like *Life Studies* and *For the Union Dead,* holding every word, phrase, and idiom up for scrutiny and still further scrutiny to the situation of an aging life.

Lowell is an important and cunning enough poet for us to venture to understand the intentions and strategies behind these *Notebook* poems. But Lowell cannot be exonerated of all blame. I would not agree with those early reviews of these books which faulted Lowell's portraits of himself,

his daughter, and his wives. For one thing, it is easy to
feel with each successive reading the reverse of what we
felt before. But, more important, the matter rests less with
the outrageousness or bad taste of the material or Lowell's
handling of it than with the sense of our having been inun-
dated by an enormous complex of feelings in the poem and
then having to sort out what those feelings, ours and
Lowell's, are. "The lines string out from nowhere, stretch
to sorrow" (*Nbk,* 177); I connected this sense of the poems
before with their capacity to seem self-generating, more
than five hundred attempts by Lowell to get things right.
What I would stress at this time relates to that flood of
sorrow which the poems proceed from and move dangerously toward.

Tellingly, Lowell refers in one of *The Dolphin* poems to
Ford's *Saddest Story* (72), the title by which Ford hoped
to call the novel which we know as *The Good Soldier.* The
connections which Lowell intends to make between Ford's
novel and his sad, novelistic, triangularly plotted poem are
clear. But whereas Ford's lyrical novel, with its infinitely
complicated, questionable narrator, is one of those works
by which we have come to know and help define modernism, Lowell's achievement in *The Dolphin,* as in *History*
and *For Lizzie and Harriet,* belongs to a very different order.
Repeatedly, Lowell's sonnets lack the distance, the variety,
and the masterly ambiguity which consistently mark Ford's
novel, "the best [and I would add, short] French novel in
the language" (*LS,* 49). They were the qualities which
marked, again consistently, the best poems of *Life Studies*
and *For the Union Dead.*

Love, and love and fame, run the risk in Lowell's recent
work of becoming heart-rending matters for the poet. They
prove as heart-rending as Lowell's wish to be younger or
eternal or god. Though sleeping or drinking with someone
makes him feel deathless, Lowell cannot, as he well knows,
have intercourse or stay drunk all the time.

History, For Lizzie and Harriet, and *The Dolphin,* considered as a single, long poem, threaten to become a tale of
sorrow which Lowell is never able to turn adequately into

lyric and love. To want to write of love, lovingly, is not necessarily to do so. To want fame is not necessarily to achieve it in art. If Lowell is guilty of anything, it is in the paraliterary standards of criticism which we are asked to take up in the reading and appreciation of the recent work. Lowell intended these *Notebook* poems to be unvanishing or some Rosetta stone for later readers to decode. To accomplish that, they have to make Lowell's life, sensibility, and reputation count inordinately.

> *Home things can't stand up to the strain of the earth*
> —Robert Lowell

What Lowell could count on from his readers in the textured, linguistically complex poems of *Life Studies* and *For the Union Dead* may not be present or forthcoming with the publication and event of Lowell's saddest story. Even *History,* while it siphons off the very personal poems into the other two volumes, has to depend upon what has happened in Lowell's own life to supply the motivating force for the book and to work against or stand behind what would otherwise often be abstract, dry poems.

In the making and accumulation of all these sonnets, Lowell lacks the saving irony which would allow the reader enough distance from the poems, enough let-up from Lowell's escalating turmoil and obsession with love and fame. When Lowell had asked in *Life Studies,* "What use is my sense of humor?", we could answer "everything," largely because we saw good evidence of it. Lowell hopes for the same advantages with these newer poems. Here is Lowell listening and talking with Harriet of Anton Webern and, by extension, himself. "What is it like? Rugged: if you can like this / you can like anything" (*FLH,* 40). But we are more likely to feel that Lowell is begging the question. And straining the comparison. The music in too many of the sonnets is not rugged or difficult at all. Earlier poems in earlier books showed Lowell helping us to penetrate and appreciate the genuinely difficult. Here, the strategy is reduced to having Lowell supply us with heavy, irresistible ammunition to gun him down.

For Sylvia Plath, in Lowell's reading of her and her art, the poems tell that the life and the art are out of control.[23] Repeatedly, it is the upheaval and confusion which Lowell has to insist upon. If we are encouraged to turn and return to his life, this is not only because of what Lowell supplies. The critical writing of Lowell's second wife, Elizabeth Hardwick, also proves central. I think of her incisive critical work, writings which are more than cool, literary endeavors and which read more like thinly disguised chapters in a life: her understanding consideration of Sylvia Plath, her meditative, sadly nostalgic impressions of Maine, her essays on seduction and betrayal in literature, her pieces on women amateurs who were great men's sisters or wives.[24] Elizabeth Hardwick has nothing of the amateur about her; she is professional in the best sense. Yet in the complex way in which she defines women "amateurs" like Dorothy Wordsworth and Jane Carlyle, we can see a fearfully prophetic connection of them with her, and we make some important link:

> A sort of insatiability seems to infect our feelings when we look back on women, particularly on those who are highly interesting and yet whose effort at self-definition through works is fitful, casual, that of an amateur. We are inclined to think they could have done more, that we can make retroactive demands upon them for a greater degree of independence and authenticity.[25]

Or here is the opening of her piece on Jane Carlyle:

> Jane Carlyle died suddenly one day, in her carriage. She

---

23. Robert Lowell, Foreword to *Ariel* (New York: Harper & Row, 1966), p. xi.

24. Elizabeth Hardwick, "On Sylvia Plath," *NYRB*, 12 August 1971, pp. 3-6; "In Maine," *NYRB*, 7 October 1971, pp. 3-6; "Amateurs: Dorothy Wordsworth & Jane Carlyle," *NYRB*, 30 November 1972, pp. 3-4; "Amateurs: Jane Carlyle," *NYRB*, 14 December 1972, pp. 32-36; "Seduction and Betrayal: I," *NYRB*, 31 May 1973, pp. 3-6; "Seduction and Betrayal II," *NYRB*, 14 June 1973, pp. 6-10.

25. Hardwick, "Amateurs," p. 3.

was sixty-five years old and had been married to Thomas Carlyle for forty years. It seems, as we look back on it, that at the moment of her death the idea was born that she had somehow been the victim of Carlyle's neglect. He thought as much and set out upon a large remorse, something like the "penance" of Dr. Johnson, although without the consolation of religion. The domestic torment the Carlyles endured in their long marriage is of a particular opacity because of the naturalness of so much of it, its origin in the mere strains of living. The conflicts were not of a remarkable kind, and domestic discontent was always complicated by other problems of termperament and by the unnerving immensity of Carlyle's literary undertakings.[26]

Phrases, turns of thought, and varied moods oddly complement some of those found in the poems of Lowell in *For Lizzie and Harriet* and *The Dolphin*. Elizabeth Hardwick's pieces on Dorothy Wordsworth and Jane Carlyle and on seduction and betrayal in literature create a passionate rhetoric which makes us connect it with the force and direction, the facts and circumstances of her own and Lowell's lives. Robert Lowell and Elizabeth Hardwick are too prominent as public, literary, and intellectual figures for us to compartmentalize his poems and her criticism.

As readers, in coming to Lowell's poems, we fill in and surround his *Notebook* poems with much that is outside and beyond literature. As Lowell's life and art risk going more and more out of control, the gaps (evident in the ellipses, printed and unprinted, in the sonnets; in those grounded, fourteenth lines; and in those sonnets or nonsonnets of more than, or less than, fourteen lines) increasingly matter. Almost in parody of some company of moderns, Lowell courts failure — to love, to write *the* long poem, to assure himself of lasting fame, to stave off old age and dying — as meaning.

---

26. Hardwick, "Amateurs," p. 32.

My art, like many others, fails. The failure is dubious.
Months of false cast, then a day, of strikes — something
happier than anything done by me before
                                            —Robert Lowell

If Lowell's two *Notebooks* gave evidence of an awareness
of Berryman's long poem, it is the gathering of *History, For
Lizzie and Harriet*, and *The Dolphin* that assures Lowell
of an inevitable comparison of his long poem with *The
Dream Songs*. For Lowell, I fear this comparison will prove
unfavorable and misleading. But I am less concerned at this
point with a judgment than with illuminating some things
in these poems which relate to my hopes and fears about
Lowell's future as a poet.

The *Dream Songs* hardly come out of a life which is in
control. Yet through the voices of Henry and Mr. Bones,
they attempt to evolve the means for managing what the
life cannot. Lowell is not unskilled in the same art. But Berryman in *The Dream Songs* writes in a lyric-elegiac style
which has already given up on some of the things in this
life and which anticipates the stylelessness of some of the
poems in *Delusions, Etc.*, like "He Resigns" and "Henry's
Understanding."[27] Unlike Berryman, Lowell still holds so
tightly to the confusions and impossibles of his and this
life that his art has not yet had time to catch up with that
life in order to find an appropriate or adequate style.

When Berryman concluded his last of the *77 Dream Songs*
(1964), the first of the two volumes which make up *The
Dream Songs*, he wrote of Henry, "with in each hand /
one of his own mad books and all," "he's making ready
to move on." And Berryman did, to a more direct style,
which brought its own pleasures and disappointments.
What is more important, however, is that, as *The Dream
Songs* changed, they came in their most telling moments
to be informed by a perspective which seems almost beyond
the reaches of life and art. Here is Berryman in one of the

27. John Berryman, *Delusions, Etc.* (New York: Farrar, Straus and
Giroux, 1972), pp. 40, 53.

late poems (no. 379) from *His Toy, His Dream, His Rest*
(1968), the second volume of *The Dream Songs:*

> Fresh toils the lightning over the Liffey, wild
> and the avenues, like Paris's, are rain
> and Henry is here for a while
> of many months, along with the squalls of a child,
> thirty years later. I will not come again
> or not come with this style.

In retrospect, the lines seem prophetic. But even without
Berryman's supporting suicide, they carry an authority
which accounts for much of the power and originality of
Berryman's long poem. They are stylized and styleless at
the same time.

And here is a passage from Lowell's poem, "Reading Myself":

> Like thousands, I took just pride and more than just,
> struck matches that brought my blood to a boil;
> I memorized the tricks to set the river on fire —
> somehow never wrote something to go back to.
>
> (H, 194)

It is similar to the Berryman passage in its assessment of
the restless need to move on. Lowell is not gainsaying his
practice of revision, a process which is central to the meaning if not the final achievement of his long work. At some
deeper level, it is part of what Lowell has done in each
succeeding book. In the poems of *Life Studies* and *For the
Union Dead* or in some of the single but major poems from
volumes as early as *Lord Weary's Castle* or as late as *Near
the Ocean*, Lowell created the impression of using the language as if he made it. However, in what began as the *Notebooks* and culminates in *History, For Lizzie and Harriet*,
and *The Dolphin*, Lowell seems unable to maintain or
manage all that he wants or intends. What I like best about
this long work are those passages which flatten out style
to accommodate a more traditional elegiac lyricism which

revision cannot help or add to significantly. Here are two
versions of one such passage:

> To summer on skidding summer, the rude spring rain
> hurries the ambitious, flowers and youth;
> the crackling flash-tone's held an hour, then we
> too follow nature, imperceptibly
> change from mouse-brown to the white lion's mane,
> to thin white, to the freckled, knuckled skull,
> bronzed by decay, by many, many suns . . .
>
>   (Nbk 67, 4)

> Spring moved to summer — the rude cold rain
> hurries the ambitious, flowers and youth;
> our flash-tones crackle for an hour, and then
> we too follow nature, imperceptibly
> change our mouse-brown to white lion's mane,
> thin white fading to a freckled, knuckled skull,
> bronzed by decay, by many, many suns . . .
>
>   (FLH, 15)

Achieved stylelessness is resistant to much or to significant
revision. When, in contrast, Lowell seeks an individuated
or less styleless style for all those *Notebook* poems which
must confront a changing, private life, he is less fortunate.
Repeatedly, that life seems too unsettled and unsettling for
the poet to write well about at all. Within the sonnet form,
no style emerges to meet or to resist the life which has dramatically moved on.

   "I see I have declined, changed, grown in recent years"
— these were Lowell's words in a 1970 symposium on the
arts, and they expressed his complex sense of how unlinear
a line artists' lives and works follow.[28] It is in this complex
sense that I would like to regard Lowell's latest work in
order to remove it from the more obvious questions of success and failure, development and reputation. My hope is

---

28. Robert Lowell, "Symposium: The Writer's Situation," *New American Review*, No. 9 (1970), 86.

that Lowell, having also "declined," will not return to this sonnet sequence but explore other forms which might also, sometimes better, help him discover a language for lyric and for love.

Chapter Two

John Berryman: "The Horror of Unlove"

It's a matter of love.

The Dream Songs make out of that potential linguistic impenetrability which always has characterized Berryman's work a thematic, dramatic center. Very early in this long poem, the "broad" in "the low bar" quips:

> "You can biff me, you can bang me, get it you'll never.
> I may be only a Polack broad but I don't lay easy.
> Kiss my ass, that's what you are." (DS no. 15)

What holds for the woman, holds for Henry (Berryman's major persona and protagonist), for the poem, and for the reader of the poem. Henry proves ornery and unappeasable. The long poem keeps refusing to yield what it is about.

The Dream Songs are distracting and distractions. They are *His Toy, His Dream, His Rest*, as Berryman indicates in the title of the second volume of poems which, together with *77 Dream Songs*, form the long work. They are distracting in other regards as well, especially in the insistence and self-consciousness from which they proceed. The 385 poems, or songs, draw attention to themselves in every possible way: by their sheer number, by their language, by their range in knowledge, thinking and feeling, and style. The poems build toward an elliptical long poem that seems unwilling to end. The poet provides Henry and his other personas with more styles than they could possibly realize or exhaust either in art or in life. Through the voices assumed in the poems, the poet becomes his own public relations man, as well as a man at the mercy of the public relations of literary reputations. Berryman, who in life could manage a loud speaking voice, finds comparable pitch and volume in many of the dream poems. The poems display the paraphernalia of mikes, broadcasts, spotlights, gramophones, P.A. systems, televisions, radios, telephones, and box-office attractions. Repeatedly, Berryman's voices are scored for bravura and brass.

Movement in *The Dream Songs* toward increasing noise is counterpointed by an alternate, sometimes concurrent movement toward understatement and silence. At this extreme, Berryman's Dream Song no. 29, "Snow Line," stands:

It was wet & white & swift and where I am
we don't know. It was dark and then
it isn't.
I wish the barker would come. There seems to be to eat
nothing. I am unusually tired.
I'm alone too.

If only the strange one with so few legs would come,
I'd say my prayers out of my mouth, as usual.
Where are his notes I loved?
There may be horribles; it's hard to tell.
The barker nips me but somehow I feel
he too is on my side.

I'm too alone. I see no end. If we could all
run, even that would be better. I am hungry.
The sun is not hot.
It's not a good position I am in.
If I had to do the whole thing over again I wouldn't.

A muted lyricism emerges here. The reduction of feeling and poetic language to the minimal gains emphasis from the image of the barker whose sideshow voice and pointer keep the personal, human world at bay. The figure and function of the barker connect with the occasions in *The Dream Songs* when Henry, middle-aged and white, is addressed as Mr. Bones. On those occasions, Berryman invokes a tradition of vaudeville or minstrelsy that utilized its straight men and interlocutors, equivalents of the barker, for keeping emotion down whenever it threatened to rise.

The impression of cool detachment which "Snow Line" conveys is due not only to the presence of the barker in the poem. For this impression, Berryman also makes use of the matter-of-fact logic of dream, a twisted and clipped syntax, and the repetition of the impersonals "it" and "there."

But "Snow Line" also creates an opposite and equally strong impression of a sentimentality that the poem's coolness, a coolness metaphorically admitted in the poem's title, seeks to evade and conceal. This impression is that beneath (above?) the snow line Berryman is writing a love poem which the piling negatives and hypothetical "if"s never succeed in overwhelming completely. The ambiguous proceedings of "Snow Line" find their analogous processes in the way dream and minstrelsy, two centers of reference and association in the poems, work. The latent and manifest content of dream, like the levels essential to the success and pleasures of minstrel blues and vaudeville traditions in art, draw near to the way Berryman manages style and sensibility in the poem.

The concluding lines of "Snow Line" may move toward an almost Sophoclean moment of thinking nonbirth best. But they never disperse a counterwill in the poem toward an acknowledgement of human need for love: warmth, rest, sustenance, music ("notes"), and light ("sun"). Berryman joins the "I" of his protagonist, Henry, in not having the option not to have been born. To have been born is the given condition and situation, as it is also the human impasse. A pathos ensues, both in the poem and in a life, from a hunger that can never, will never be realized adequately. "Supreme my holdings, greater yet my need," Berryman begins his dream song no. 64.

The moment which Berryman records in the lines, "The barker nips me but somehow I feel / he too is on my side," depends upon an aesthetic of pathos. It is the kind of aesthetic which writers like Saul Bellow and J. D. Salinger often make prominent in their work. Henderson and Herzog, like Holden and Franny, experience radical crises in feeling not unlike moments in Henry's life. That Berryman dedicated his *77 Dream Songs* to Bellow (along with Kate, Berryman's third wife) acknowledges more than a personal friendship. A matter of common sensibilities also surfaces. Berryman's habit or preference — what Robert Mazzocco has called "the heart-shaped irony"[1] — at times shares more with writers of prose like Bellow and Salinger than with some of the modern poets, whose kinship with Berryman, in the end, may be of a less telling kind.

Beyond analogies with the sensibilities of other contemporaries, however, such a moment in "Snow Line" establishes a connection with moments in Shakespeare's *King Lear*. In particular, one moment comes to mind:

The little dogs and all,
Tray, Blanch, and Sweetheart, see, they bark at me.
(III. vi. 65-66)

"The barker" in Berryman's "Snow Line" might be meant to recall this moment in the play. One of Berryman's intended projects was a critical edition of *King Lear,* and the connection with a moment so telling in the play and in a play Berryman was so familiar with would not be impossible.[2] But, in the end, to cite the Shakespearean passage

---

1. Robert Mazzocco, "Harlequin in Hell," *The New York Review of Books,* 29 June 1967, p. 12. Hereafter, references to this journal will be given as *NYRB.*

2. Jane Howard, "Whisky and Ink, Whisky and Ink," *Life Magazine,* 21 July 1967, p. 75. See also Robert Lowell, "The Poetry of John Berryman," *NYRB,* 28 May 1964, p. 3.

in order to assign to "the barker" another meaning (little dog) is less important than to establish what these moments in Shakespeare and Berryman have in common: the expression of the need to work back to feeling, however strange or diminutive, imaginary or ambiguous a form this sense of community momentarily might take. The pathetic moment, if evasive, also can signal the way back.

The coolness as well as an excess of sentiment that I observed in "Snow Line" becomes apparent in moments at the other extreme of that poem, in poems of intense activity and brass:

> He took a hard look
> at the programme of the years
> and struck his hardened palms across his ears
> & 'Basta!' cried: I should have been a noted crook
> or cat in a loud slum yes.
>
> (No. 343)

This Dream Song and "Snow Line" end by containing within them the same contradictory directions of intense emotion and calm.

As the dream songs alternate between manic and depressive maneuvers, perhaps a modern equivalent of Thomas Nashe's "queerly schizophrenic" style,[3] Berryman complicates both extremes by similar, paradoxical impressions. But a note, which will prove a leitmotif for the poems, keeps demanding to be heard, "it's a matter of love" (no. 372). Or, as Berryman expresses it in another poem, "Working & children & pals are the point of the thing" (no. 303). Poems, children, and friends are drawn into loving alignment and explicitly so.

Berryman composes out of a love which never seems adequate to or in expression. At times, this love takes on the sexual-aesthetic dimensions of the work of Walt Whit-

3. John Berryman, Introduction to Thomas Nashe, *The Unfortunate Traveller; or, The Life of Jack Wilton,* ed. John Berryman (New York: G. P. Putnam's Sons, 1960), p. 12.

man or Hart Crane. Significantly, these poets are among
the artists most prominent throughout the dream songs.

"It's a matter of love." But Berryman uses every imagin-
able device to deflect that fact, however simpler the syntax
of the later poems became. The poet gains distance by
proceedings that assume the force of a method and a dialectic. The poems, as "Snow Line" evidenced, insist upon
coming to their world obliquely. The poet distances his material through the persona of Henry and, in turn, through
Henry's ability to shift person and voice, face and style;
through lending things the impersonality of anecdote and
bad joke and tale; and through devoting whole poems or
strategic portions of poems to forestalling criticism of *The
Dream Songs* as a long poem.

Berryman also, ironically, achieves distance by "letting
out" so much love that a reader or audience has no option
at times but to seek invisibility. Pathetic, bathetic moments
create their own spaces of reserve, whether or not the poet
chooses to point the way back to feeling and however much
or little he may feel called on to help. Sometimes, in the
course of a poem, Berryman is able to move beyond a
heart-rending plea for a "vision of friendlies" to discover
a more acceptable and finally more moving lyricism:

Of heartless youth made late aware he pled:
Brownies, please come.
To Henry in his sparest times sometimes
the little people spread, & did friendly things:
then he was glad.

. . . .
Please, please
come.

My friends, — he has been known to mourn, — I'll die;
live you, in the most wild, kindly, green
partly forgiving wood,
sort of forever and all those human sings
close not your better ears to, while good Spring

returns with a dance and a sigh.

(No. 27)

Sometimes Berryman's rapid reversals in feeling assure for
him the reception of feeling that would otherwise have been
dispersed and disposed of, once it was entertained:

Gongs & lightning crowd my returned throat,
I always wept at parades: I knew I'd fail:
Henry wandered back on stage & sat.

(No. 257)

Sometimes the unbearable things asked of the "I" of Henry
are embraced and turned away, admitted and willed transparent at the same time:

The sudden sun sprang out

I gave the woman & her child ten shillings,
I can't bear beggars at my door, and I
cannot bear at my door
the miserable, accusing me, and sore
back to my own country would I go
transparent, through the sky.

(No. 378)

This poem, proceeding from a stay by Berryman in Ireland,
moves toward the universality of need. At home or abroad,
Berryman addresses what is a recurrent dilemma for him
as a needy, wanting poet and man.

Berryman's deflection in the dream songs, then, is not
what it might first seem. Evasive poetic ways never completely disguise feeling which the poet often gives the impression of trying to skirt. Attempts at evading feeling by
using minstrel blackface and impersonal, slangy idioms work
both ambiguously and not ambiguously at all: "— You is
from hunger, Mr Bones," Berryman writes in Dream Song
no. 76. The very vulnerability and need, intended for denial,
not only are admitted but underlined. Vaudeville turns,

introduced to create distance, in part bridge that distance
and even can conclude by becoming "hellish." Related to
this method, Henry's tales, started about someone else, end
by being about a first-person Henry: "So. / I am her" (no.
242). In another song, the displacement involved in casting
intense moments into story form may go undetected at first
glance:

> Dogs fill daylight, doing each other ill:
> my own in love was lugged so many blocks
> we had to have a vet.

(No. 106)

But as the poem drives on to its conclusion, there is no
doubt of Berryman's intentions. What began as an uncomfortable, ugly tale is transformed into a series of questionings
on love: whether "lustful" love is inevitable; whether "hurt-
less love" exists; whether "grace" can or should withstand
the animal in man. Momentarily, in dream songs like these,
Berryman draws near to those emotions which, first and
last, motivate the poems. Such occasions were less available
to the Berryman of the *Sonnets*. In those early poems,
Berryman also was engaged in "crumpling a syntax at a
sudden need."[4] But the syntax of the *Sonnets* seldom un-
folded the emotions they so artfully sought to contain.

The distinctiveness of *The Dream Songs* resides in how
the crises in feeling recorded by the poet have to be dealt
with, moment by moment, as artfully as the poet knows
how. Berryman's Henry sheds more tears in the poems than
any one lifetime could produce. Handkerchiefs recur as real,
useful objects and as props. Simultaneously, Henry's tear
ducts are "worn out" and inexhaustible at their source of
grief. But Henry Pussycat is not ordinary, and Berryman's
responses to the world, as a human being and as a poet,
uncover sadness everywhere. The poems break off, resume,

---

4. John Berryman, Sonnet 47, *Berryman's Sonnets* (New York: Farrar,
Straus and Giroux, 1967), p. 47. Hereafter, other references to *Berryman's Sonnets* will be included in the text and given by sonnet number.

only to give way to the welling up of new feeling. Recurrently, emotion gives the impression of beginning in medias res:
"Thrums up from nowhere a distinguisht wail, / The griefs
of all his grievous friends, and his" (no. 334). The abrupt
entry which many of the poems in Lowell's Life Studies
relied upon functions as an even more extreme stratagem
in Berryman. So immediate can this sense become, that, even
after a poem has begun, Berryman could write: "Starts again
always in Henry's ears / the little cough somewhere, an
odour, a chime" (no. 29). Yet if feeling emerges, the larger
question of feeling in the body of the long poems is a less
simple matter.

Intensity and immediacy are as much in evidence in The
Dream Songs as they are absent. Tears for the world and
for the sufferings of the individuals of that world fall and
exhaust themselves less often than they "almost fall." In
the end, the "grievously understated" griefs of Henry prove
more typical of him.

In response to the question, "— How are you?" Berryman
supplies, "— Fine, fine. (I have tears unshed," (no. 207). The
response is a telling one. "Tears unshed" suggests tears still
to be shed. However, by the use of parenthesis and inversion, Berryman creates an extreme metaphor of tears taken
back into the body, as if in parody of the reversibility of
the rain cycle arrowed in by children in early science classes.

Tears, whether shed or unshed, keep before a reader the
realization that Berryman's dream songs, all 385 of them,
proceed out of a lyrical center. While this center commonly
acknowledges other modes (satiric, dramatic, narrative,
epic), the poems in their deepest commitments are lyric.
And the lyricism derives from a burden of need which
depends upon love for its realization and fulfillment.

"Need" and "love" are among the most insistent words
and foci in The Dream Songs. They are as insistent as Lear's
"no"s and "nothing"s, and as pathetic as some of the later
moments in that play where "need" and "love" also figure
so centrally. Berryman writes:

Love me love me love me love me love me

I am in need thereof, I mean of love.

(No. 192)

Hunger was constitutional with him,
women, cigarettes, liquor, need need need
until he went to pieces.

(No. 311)

Need and love extend beyond the particular contexts to
assume dimensions which are archetypal. An urgency appears in these songs which the *Short Poems* and the *Sonnets*
noticeably lacked. Berryman frequently associates "needing
Henry" with his protagonist's capacity as lover or would-be
lover. The notes are familiar ones:

And will love last
further than tonight?

(No. 313)

& where are the moments of love?

(No. 343)

Need is never satisfied. "Enough" is meaningless.

also, also, somehow.
. . . .
and needed more.

(No. 90)

too much was never enough.

(No. 351)

Such notes, if in danger of sounding trite, appear more moving in the contexts of particular poems and in the context
of a life filled with impasses.

Considerations of love and need caused Berryman to raise
questions that are at once abstract and intensely personal.
Again, I am reminded of *King Lear,* whose set speeches and

asides on "love" and "need" provide some of the more emotional and metaphysical moments in that play. By means of the many voices of Henry, Berryman is able to play not only Lear, but Cordelia with her father. In the course of *The Dream Songs,* Berryman creates more complications about matters of need and love than he can ever begin to untangle. Henry worries over relentless contradictions within and without himself. He probes the deception of need. He knows love's costs. Fears attack him regarding his capacity to love. The worries prove both private and philosophical.

Berryman shifts Henry's fear for his ability or capacity to love into third-person gossip and accusation, "They say Henry's love is well beyond Henry" (no. 269). Henry's fear nicely complicates itself. Fear or boast? Is Henry inadequate to love or does Henry's love have some kind of final, self-emptying and transcendent nature? The ironies of the line are never decided. Behind such ironies lie unending questionings, abstract disquisitions and private agonies, about Henry's and John Berryman's love. Berryman's ladder of love in *The Dream Songs* proves a complicated one. "All degrees of love" (no. 255) tax him. "Nothing loving is alien to me," Berryman's Henry might well have sung.

The love against which Henry is measured by others measures himself, and the love toward which he aspires accounts for terrifying exactions. Christ's association with "the death of the death of love" (no. 48) intrigues Berryman. Poems that link Henry and God-as-Christ are obsessively filled with Christ, specifically as the New Testament God of Love. Such a connection leads Berryman to speculations which address contradiction and paradox at every turn, both for Henry and for Christ. How and when is sacrifice ever pure? How can one reconcile a figure of great love with situations and results which often speak of lovelessness? Berryman's painful ironies of love lie close to the heart of the poem. Out of meditative, dramatic discoursings on love and need, Berryman makes a relentless quest. In that effort as a poet, he touches on what is needed and given, wanted and returned. He does this on a scale suggestive of paranoia, a paranoia that "calls for this thud of love from his creatures-O" (no. 238).

Henry's worries regarding love continually partake of a reductive simplicity: "He wondered: Do I love?" Berryman writes in Dream Song no. 118. Yet the questions raised by the question are neither reductive nor simple. Instead, Berryman assigns to "the concept 'love'" (no. 160) a weight and an intensity that are inordinate. Such extreme burdens are placed upon love that Berryman significantly surrounds it, as word and as concept, with quotation marks. In the case of the deaths of his father and his friend, Delmore Schwartz, to whose "sacred memory" *His Toy, His Dream, His Rest* is dedicated, Berryman's love is so overwhelming in what it would give and in what it needs to be sufficient that it almost "dies" from him. The rhetoric proves to be more than a stylistic device. It represents a typical, defining movement in all of Berryman's work. Commonly, in the guise of a negative syntax or dialectic Berryman sets down his most mystical, loving words.

In his need to love and be loved, Berryman's Henry must confront the limitations of himself as a desiring man. He must also confront the limitations of that man in a world where need and realized desire seldom are one. As the dilemma of Everyman, it takes on the look of epigraph for the entire body of poems: "There ought to be a law against Henry. / — Mr. Bones: there is" (no. 4). Here, in a tellingly distanced blackface, Berryman approaches one of the informing centers of the poems. It stands as close to Berryman's sense of things as a passage in *Troilus and Cressida* stands to Shakespeare's view of the human impasse:

> This is the monstrosity in love, lady, that the will is infinite and the execution confined; that the desire is boundless and the act a slave to limit.
>
> (III.ii.86-90)

But epigraph need not be epitaph unless a writer chooses it to be so.

For Berryman, an acknowledgement of "overneeds," the

need for "extra love" or "surplus love," causes him not to abandon man in the contradictions that surround him. Instead, Berryman begins where he can begin, with what defines man and makes him unique, his capacity for language and love. Love may not last, and need may linger on. But this does not stop Berryman from loving and "versing." Out of this situation. *The Dream Songs* proceed, like self-generated love songs or "Valentines." What the poet seeks is the creation of a community of caring friends, men and women who will share with him their talk and love.

One of the most moving moments in *The Dream Songs* occurs in no. 255, where Berryman relates the tale of the child in Henry's (his own?) daughter's kindergarten class. It is Valentine's Day and, in the classroom exchange of cards, his child receives no Valentine. In the most basic way, the entire corpus of Dream Songs is written to supply that card.

That the Dream Songs are love poems becomes most obvious in the lyric-linguistic bias of Berryman's work. In the elegies and "*Op. posth.*" pieces, Berryman insistently links the figure of poet and lover. Love and expression are one.

In *Homage to Mistress Bradstreet,* Berryman had given Anne the words, "vellum I palm."[5] Versing in *The Dream Songs* also joins the sexual to the aesthetic. Berryman's numerous memorial poems link the "heart" and "art" of love; his rhyming "heart" and "art" functions as instructively as his "need" and "seed" does in other contexts. The poet-figures Berryman eulogizes in his poems are remembered for writing well, for crafting poems as an act of love. Translators and translations also become, respectively, workers and works of love.

Berryman joins himself in *The Dream Songs* to poets like W. C. Williams and Randall Jarrell, Delmore Schwartz and Sylvia Plath. These poets, as Berryman views them, also made "a good sound" out of love. That poet-critics like Robert Lowell and William Meredith have written some of the

---

5. John Berryman, *Homage to Mistress Bradstreet* (New York: Farrar, Straus and Cudahy, 1956), st. 10, 1. 1, n.p.

best criticism of Berryman reveals similar connections. Such men entered into the loving, writing community which Berryman so desperately came to depend upon. The community of caring friends which Berryman established in *Homage to Mistress Bradstreet* between himself and that one poet is infinitely enlarged in *The Dream Songs* to range more freely among countries, cultures, and centuries; and this community intently seeks comfort in numbers. A majority of one ceases to be enough.

Each Dream Song makes a new attempt at expression and love. Berryman never deceives himself about the labor involved. He knows the risky attractiveness of silence and refuses to turn *The Dream Songs* into dejection odes. Although Berryman considers and names himself among the company of poets like Coleridge (no. 12), he stops short of that "last victory" dejection ode which, as Frank Kermode, writing on the English Romantic poet, points out, also "exhausts him."[6] Berryman uncannily is able to acknowledge a kinship with a poet like Coleridge without embracing that silence which has always represented for the poet, even before the Romantics, the temptation of a kind of death. But this is the Berryman of *The Dream Songs;* the later poems and books and suicide are still to come.

In his elegy on Roethke (no. 18), Berryman envies Roethke for gaining in death a freedom from the excessive cost of art and love demanded of the poet-lover:

No more daily, trying to hit the head on the nail:
thirstless: without a think in his head:
back from wherever, with it said.

But envy of Roethke in death, reminiscent of Anne Sexton's envy of Sylvia Plath's end,[7] does not prevent Berryman from writing on. The cost of love and art, if not welcomed,

---

6. Frank Kermode, *Romantic Image* (London: Routledge and Kegan Paul, 1957), p. 11.

7. Anne Sexton, "Sylvia's Death," *Live or Die* (Boston: Houghton Mifflin, 1966), pp. 38-40.

is accepted as part of the poet's trade.

In arts other than poetry, Berryman also accepts the human and superhuman effort exacted of the artist. Of the painter Renoir,[8] Berryman says:

> "I paint"
> (Renoir said) "with my penis."
>
> (No. 221)

Neither the third-person reportage nor the innocent bawdry of the remark disguises the link to which Berryman draws our attention — that of art and of love.

Whether Berryman's poetic expression in *The Dream Songs* will be adequate merges into fears for his sexual potency. Mikes, gramophones, telephones, pens, and pencils link the instrument of expression or communication with phallic strength and length. Berryman's Henry alternately boasts and fears for his sexual-aesthetic self:

> my gramophone is the most powerful in the country.
>
> (No. 204)

> we'll cut off his telephone.
>
> (No. 350)

In the course of *The Dream Songs* no humor is too indecorous for Berryman, whose habit of sexual punning becomes notorious: "whole," "country," "come," "lay," "piece," "stub point," "Venus." But Berryman's puns seldom are indulgent. They often return the reader to what is an important center in the poems. "Venus" can be both Goddess of Love and brand of pencil. "Lay" can be both song and "lovely fuck." Berryman manages to pass so effortlessly from love to art or from woman to poem that the two continually merge, sometimes happily, into one: "a medium where 'Fuck you' comes as no curse / but come as

---

8. Berryman attributes the remark to Lautrec. See John Berryman, *Recovery* (New York: Farrar, Straus and Giroux, 1973), p. 9. Hereafter, references to *Recovery (R)* will be included in the text.

a sigh or a prayer" (no. 227). "Curse" proves to be blessing;
"medium" proves to be sexual and aesthetic at the same
time.

In some very intimate way, Berryman may remind the
reader of the Calvinist who, although finally uncertain of
salvation, must go on to act as if he were to be among the
saved. Berryman wrote *The Dream Songs,* aware of the contradictions and ambiguities of man and of man's art. That,
in the end, Henry and the poet never can match love to
need, except in those brief moments of loving and versing,
helps to explain a good deal about the work: its length; the
poet's unwillingness to conclude; the danger of the poet's
repeating himself by writing poems that, again and again,
must satisfy the same needs. Similarly, the cost involved
in that effort helps to explain the continuing distractions
along the way: the quirky syntax, extreme topical references
and the range of styles included in the poems. That "it's
a matter of love" at once is a consoling and frightening fact.
As the syntax in the later songs becomes less twisted, the
continuing concern of the poet with loving and versing
proves either too obvious or not obvious enough.

Berryman knows how annoying and wily he and his
poems can be. His extended use of the image of the Viet
Cong who will not be brought into camp (no. 333) extends
both to himself and to the reader, who, he fears, will not
accept the terms of the poems. In the phrase, brought "into
camp," Berryman expresses in pun an awareness of the kind
of sensibility the poems border on. But we ought not to
be fooled. The poems, if at times approaching the style of
camp, also enable the reader not to miss the very feeling
the poet seeks to hide. Berryman's hell is a very real hell,
as are his happier fields. We must not become the bad critic
who mistakes where the real preferences of the poems lie:

They'll seek the strange soul, in rain & mist,
whereas they should recall the pretty cousins they kissed,
and stick with the sweet switch of the body.

                                                    (No. 308)

Berryman does more than playfully caution us here. He is didactic in his advice.

But such a moment, in the end, is not typical. More often, the poems do their utmost to lead us astray. Even the less clotted poems of *His Toy, His Dream, His Rest* have their own ways of putting a reader off. Always, the poet utilizes a proliferation of objects, places, and names. Berryman's "prone for products" is at once personal, American, and part of an American literary-philosophical tradition of empiricism to which many of the poems of earlier poets like Whitman, Williams, Pound, and Stevens belong.

The effort which Berryman asks of the reader in *The Dream Songs* is enormous. To linger too long among the cities, however holy, or among the arts or religions that attach to them, is a danger continually offered by the poems. But the reader must learn to avoid this distraction in order to see where the real center lies:

"Kyoto, Toledo,
Benares — the holy cities —
and Cambridge shimmering do not make up
for, well, the horror of unlove,
nor south from Paris driving in the Spring
to Siena and on ..."

(No. 74)

"The horror of unlove." To move from "unlove" to love — this is what these poems are all about. The prefix "un-" recurs throughout the poems. It proves symptomatic both of how the poems proceed and how they must be read (unread?). Dream Song no. 45 ends with "un-". Berryman's "un-" is functional for the poem in which it occurs. But, even more important, it is symbolic of the kinds of seemingly contractory movements and maneuvers which take place in so many of the poems.

A related complication occurs in Berryman's concurrent mocking and acceptance of the footnotes that critics, from hostile, professional critics to Ph.D. dissertation writers, set against the poems:

His foes are like footnotes, he figured, sought
chiefly by doctoral candidates: props, & needed, —
comic relief, — absurd.

(No. 352)

Footnotes are seen as unnecessary and necessary, comic and
absurd. Berryman uses footnotes in order to gain distance
and protection. Similar considerations fill the last stanza
of Dream Song no. 373 and with a reminder of earlier connections which I noted in the songs:

will assistant professors become associates
by working on his works?

Berryman has it both ways. He satirizes the academy. And
he puns on "associates" as associate professors and as loving, caring community of friends. Once more, he returns
to what even the most extreme obfuscations would hide,
an unending expression of love. And for that business,
repeated over and over, who could be better equipped than
the poet as ideal man?

She never undertook to know
What death with love should have to doe
—Richard Crashaw

Lyric by loving lyric, *The Dream Songs* proceed. As separate poems. Yet in the process, Berryman simultaneously
moves toward the creation of a long poem, *the* long poem
to the extent that his intentions, ambition, and craft will
allow. The second volume of the songs, *His Toy, His Dream,
His Rest,* reveals increasing attention given to the progress
and process of what Berryman has chosen to take on. The
procedure assumes the enormity of a life work in art. It
is as if, and I quote from a very early, pre-Dream Songs
poem, "the words here are / At work upon salvation.[9]

9. John Berryman, "Caravan," *Short Poems* (New York: Farrar, Straus
and Giroux, 1967), p. 21.

Berryman lends to " 'The Care & Feeding of Long Poems' " the force of a thematic, dramatic center. An entire poem, Dream Song no. 354, is devoted to the subject, and Berryman forgoes no opportunity to remind his readers of his large intentions for the work. Echoes of moments in Pound's *Hugh Selwyn Mauberley* and of the beginning of Ginsberg's *Howl*, Part I, lend to *The Dream Songs* resonance and breadth:

> ". . . as for literature
> "It gives no man a sinecure.
>
> "And no one knows, at sight, a masterpiece.
> "And give up verse, my boy,
> "There's nothing in it."
>
> The "Nineties" tried your game
> And died, there's nothing in it.[10]
>
> I've given up literature & taken down pills.
>
> (No. 107)
>
> I saw the best minds of my generation destroyed by
>   madness, starving hysterical naked.[11]
>
> I'm cross with god who has wrecked this generation.
> First he seized Ted, then Richard [R. P. Blackmur],
>   Randall, and now Delmore.
> In between he gorged on Sylvia Plath.
>
> (No. 153)

The context of the Pound passage, the "Mr. Nixon" poem where Arnold Bennett is giving advice, is as important as the relationship of the first Berryman passage to Berryman's

---

10. Ezra Pound, "Mr. Nixon," *Hugh Selwyn Mauberley, Personae* (New York: Boni & Liveright, 1926), pp. 67-68.

11. Allen Ginsberg, "Howl," *Howl and Other Poems* (San Francisco: City Lights Books, 1956), p. 9.

long work.[12] Just as Pound does not have his genuine poet
in Part I of *Mauberley* give in either to a post-Nineties' decadence or to the time-serving advice of Bennett, so Berryman
resists during the duration of *The Dream Songs* impulses
toward suicide and silence. The situation recorded in the
second set of quotations indicates related connections and
strategies. Both Ginsberg and Berryman attest to the very
situation, that of loss, which their own long poems are set
against.

Berryman places himself in that long line of American
poets who also wrote long poems: Whitman, Crane, Pound
Eliot Stevens and Williams. Pound's "MAKE IT NEW" and
Williams's "Invent" consciously figure in Berryman's long
poem:

MAKE IT NEW

. . . .
Day by day make it new[13]

For years then I forgot you [Yeats], I put you down,
ingratitude is the necessary curse
of making things new.

                                                    (No. 312)

Compose. (No ideas
but in things) Invent![14]

The moneys & the tummy grew to a gale

---

12. *Hugh Selwyn Mauberley* may also have been on Berryman's mind
in *Love & Fame*; Berryman's themes and his use of stanzas in *Love
& Fame* may have important debts to this Pound poem. For this argument, see William H. Pritchard, review of *Love & Fame, The New York
Times Book Review,* 24 January 1971, p. 5.

13. Ezra Pound, Canto 53, *Cantos* (New York: New Directions, 1972),
p. 265. Pound also took *Make It New* as the title for one collection
of his essays; see Ezra Pound, *Make It New* (London: Faber and Faber,
1934).

14. William Carlos Williams, "A Sort of a Song," *The Collected Later
Poems of William Carlos Williams,* rev. ed. (New York: New Directions,
1963), p. 7.

   wafting him onward where he would not ail
   but invent endlessly.

(No. 328)

We find Pound's "MAKE IT NEW" and Williams's "Invent" as much a part of an Imagist program as a part of what their long poems complexly intend. Significantly, the use of such phrases can be found throughout their life's work, behind short poem and long poem alike, and in both cases far beyond the more limited aims of Imagism. Although Berryman's Dream Song no. 312 is about Yeats and Yeats's achievements, Berryman is able, through the phrase, "MAKE IT NEW," to link Yeats and Pound (once secretary to Yeats), and to establish a correspondence between Berryman's and Pound's efforts at lyric and long poem.

   Berryman's concern in writing a long American poem determines many concerns within the work. These are concerns which both join him to and separate him from the poet of the *Cantos*. Berryman reveals in *The Dream Songs* several things: a large fund of Puritanical guilt; a search for an adequate tradition and for ancestors; a preoccupation with "know-how" and with the "labour" that never seems to get done. Berryman's "labour" and "know-how" — also referred to in Berryman's long poem as "work," "craft," "song," "costs," "rhyme," "toils," and "art" — function as more than therapy or deflection, as more than a Beckett-like way of using up days and nights. Work, for Berryman, the born Catholic, amounts to nothing less than Puritan exorcism and prayer.

   Berryman complicates a particularly American thrust in the poem by an extension of his work not only to a European and Western humanistic past, but to an Eastern culture he finds attractive as a sensibility and as an art form. A sense of an American West and South and their folk history does not prevent Berryman from acknowledging the Western world of Greek and Roman epic, drama, and dance. Berryman can move his protagonist Henry among images of Davy Crockett, Daddy Rice, Achilles, Philoctetes, Odysseus, and Aeneas. Similarly, Berryman's Henry simulta-

neously can embrace American East Coast idiom and Eastern Buddha stance.

What Berryman seems to intend for *The Dream Songs*
is the stature of a work that can manage national and international naive and elitist styles.[15] Berryman's pun in
Dream Song no. 318 reveals several things: "and Henry's
work, on the Atlantic Shelf / will begin to disappear." "Atlantic Shelf" draws attention not only to ocean ledge and
bookshelf but to the ways in which this long work challenges the critic who seeks to find a tradition for the poem.
How the poem should be judged became an obsessive concern for Berryman. Sections of poems hammer away at the
would-be critic, and Dream Song no. 308 explicitly calls itself "An Instruction to Critics." In the *Sonnets,* Berryman
had also seen the problems involved in the ability or inability of criticism to handle innovative, long works:

> They'll say "I wonder
> What is in Berryman lately? I find him stranger
> Than usual" — working their nickel in the slot
> They'll try again, dreamless they drag from yonder
> Vexed to my leather chair this lathered ranger
>
> (Sonnet 84)

Both in the *Sonnets* and *The Dream Songs,* Berryman's worries look very much like a "Tradition and the Individual
Talent" argument conducted and constructed in verse.

Berryman's ambitions for *The Dream Songs* as epic work
raise considerations not unlike those of Williams's *Paterson*
or Lowell's *Life Studies* or *Notebook* poems. In all these
works, there are epic dimensions, just as there are narrative,
satiric, and dramatic modes. Yet, in the end, it is as lyric
or lyric sequences that these poems most profoundly proceed and succeed, if they succeed at all.[16]

---

15. Gabriel Pearson, "John Berryman: Poet as Medium," *The Review,*
No. 15 (1965), 15.

16. M. L. Rosenthal, *The New Poets: American and British Poetry
Since World War II* (New York: Oxford University Press, 1967), p. 20.
See also M. L. Rosenthal, "Dynamics of Form and Motive in Some Repre-

Despite Berryman's use of "Books" and some of the machinery of epic, his long poem continually makes its way and creates its impact by means of lyrical images of loss and love.[17] Successful individual poems stand more autonomously than Berryman might have intended. Lyric power is most in evidence, while Berryman struggles with the epic unity of the work.

Berryman's Henry, "hero, malgre lui" (no. 70) connects more with the recurrent persona of the " 'ineffectual failure,' " or "hero manqué" or "poète maudit." These are figures more familiar to us from personas in the lyrics of Lowell[18] than from any hero we might ever encounter in classical or Christian epic.

More tellingly, Berryman's company includes Swift, Coleridge, Keats, Rilke, Whitman, Hardy, Yeats, Joyce, Strindberg, Benn, and Housman. They are all lyrical talents and mentioned recurrently in *The Dream Songs*. They are closer to Berryman in sensibility than are writers who worked exclusively in epic or satiric or narrative modes.

The lyrical center of *The Dream Songs*, once located, brings with it considerable problems for the poet and for the reader. The intensities and compressions which involve Berryman commonly result in creating an impression of an impersonal, lyric voice. As with Berryman's ambitions for *The Dream Songs* as epic work, his lyricism runs the risk of pushing language more and more to the foreground at the expense of whatever was to be done or said or sung.

Part of Berryman's dilemma in his long poem derives from a continuing attempt to move toward some pure, ultimate song:

17. For an interesting consideration of the book structure and song number(s) in *The Dream Songs* in terms of numerology, see Jerome Mazzarro, "Berryman's Dream World," *The Kenyon Review*, 31, No. 124 (1969), 259-63. See also Anon., "The Life of the Modern Poet," review of *Delusions, Etc., The Times Literary Supplement*, 23 February 1973, p. 194.

18. Jerome Mazzarro, *The Poetic Themes of Robert Lowell* (Ann Arbor: The University of Michigan Press, 1965), p. 110. See also Rosenthal, *The New Poets*, pp. 48, 59.

ha, and we are pitched toward the last love,
the last dream, the last song.

(No. 137)

You go by the rules but there the rules don't matter
is what I've been trying to say.

(No. 204)

Henry his horns waved at the future of poetry, where
he had been.

(No. 208)

making them [the audience] wonder what's missing,
a strangeness in the final notes, never to be resolved.

(No. 331)

The attraction to some kind of final poetry Berryman often
expresses in analogies from music and painting, definitively
nonverbal media. And, beyond that, he links such poetry
with those moments or achievements in music and painting
which seem to him most extreme in their accomplishment,
the accomplishment of notes or brush-strokes almost
beyond the human reaches of art — the particular intensities
of Mozart and Beethoven, Van Gogh and Renoir. Berryman
knows the costly effort of his undertaking and of the undertaking of all major, absolute art. His man Henry self-
consciously voices fear for the genius and patience needed
to record that final song — "but can Henry write it?" (no.
103).

Berryman's program for The Dream Songs is at once inclusive and exclusive. It is exclusive in its content and in
the elitist, Yeatsean audience it imagines. It is inclusive to
the point of having Berryman wish nothing or no one, living
or dead, escape from the work. This inclusiveness, instead
of being comforting, turns into a nightmare of proliferation
where, after endless ledgering, Berryman lets no one go:

But never did Henry, as he thought he did,
end anyone and hacks her body up

and hide the pieces, where they may be found.
He knows: he went over everyone, & nobody's missing.
Often he reckons, in the dawn, them up.
Nobody is ever missing.

(No. 29)

With echoes of *Sweeney Agonistes*, Berryman counters
with his own dream vision because of its nightmare of
deathlessness more horrible than Eliot's.

Whether *The Dream Songs* can sustain itself as a long,
lyrical poem about the horror of unlove wars with tenden-
cies toward autonomy in the work. While love and language
are intimately related, Berryman never disposes of the
dangers of decadence: confusions of art and life, death and
love. The center of the poem is lyrical and linguistic, perhaps too insistently so:

Father being the loneliest word in the one language.

(No. 241)

Berryman's discriminating awareness and admission that
English is only "one language" still do not prevent the incipient decadence of the line and of much of the poem. "Father" as word threatens to engulf "father" as father.

The risks of language replacing life never disperse themselves completely in *The Dream Songs*. Like the novelist
identifying with the obituary dead (no. 53), Berryman's
Henry is too adept at emphathizing with and re-creating
the dead. "Henry House" links wood and word and word
and world to the point of dangerous confusion:

My wood or word seems to be rotting.

(No. 85)

My house is made of wood and it's made well.

(No. 385)

At times, instead of reverting to Berryman, the construct which we encounter as *The Dream Songs* looks like an inadequate, deflective substitute for life. We find Henry at one point in the songs deserting life for art:

> Leaving the known world with an awkward kiss
> he haunted, back among his colleagues in this verse
> constructed in angry play.
>
> (No. 178)

It is not that Berryman is unaware of the dangers of an implicit, marginal decadence. The humor he can manage in its face can be considerable; "A stub point: one odd way to Paradise," Berryman wrote in Dream Song no. 261. But in many of the other songs there is less of a conscious, real struggle between the claims of art and life. Too often pen threatens to replace penis. Love and life tend to be kept at too comfortable and safe a distance. What begins as a humorous retelling of a story barely hides what is occurring, namely art replacing sex as source and organ:

> They wanted to know whether his sources of inspiration
> might now be Irish: I cried out "of course"
> & waved him off with my fountain pen.
>
> (No. 342)

In the earlier poems from *77 Dream Songs*, Berryman also was obsessed with fears of castration in life and through art. "They took away his crotch" (no. 8) is both a nightmarish fear of impotency and a suspicion that the poet could be violated by art, whether that art be good or bad, dangerous or kind.

In *The Dream Songs* Berryman's language frequently suffers from the masturbatory indulgence we meet in characters and in the language of characters, in Genet and Albee, in Bellow and Salinger and Roth. The other three poets I am considering in this book present dangers and instances of the same kind. In all these writers' works, language moves toward replacing love and life — action, character, speech. Berryman's wish for "massage at all hours" (no. 351) rivals that of one of the figures in Sylvia Plath's "Death & Co.":

Bastard
Masturbating a glitter
He wants to be loved.[19]

In this way, the persons or the words of Roth's Portnoy or of Albee's Martha and George might be described.

Berryman, by giving language a more and more prominent place in his work, necessarily commits himself to the risks of leaving out or obscuring feeling. It is that fund of feeling which major poetry must somehow manage to embrace. From the Sonnets to The Dream Songs, Berryman's "words," or "mots," "fly." The Sonnets, although written about an actual affair, exceed the sonneteers' conventional attention to his poor, inadequate art. And The Dream Songs turn a traditional concern of the poet with language into an obsessive, even pathological motif. In theory, the world which Berryman wishes to create in his long poem sounds at once reasonable and ambitious: "the construction of a world rather than the reliance upon one which is available to a small poem."[20] Considering the achievement of 77 Dream Songs, the first volume of Berryman's long work, the critic Gabriel Pearson found something very much like what Berryman intended:

Berryman has had the courage not to inhibit his linguistic self-consciousness but to develop it to the full. By adding voice to voice, simulation to simulation, he has succeeded in creating a viable body of experience. This experience is the assemblage of voices itself, a complex of attitudes, tones, tunes, and styles which add up, as it were, to the

---

19. Sylvia Plath, "Death & Co.," Ariel (New York: Harper & Row, 1966), p. 28.

20. John Berryman, "One Answer to a Question," Shenandoah, 17, No. 1 (1965), 75-76.

density of a life. Or, perhaps, is beginning to.[21]

Yet both Berryman's plan for his long poem and Pearson's criticism look like an apology for a decadent aesthetics: life existing and aiming to end in a book.

Just as Berryman deftly passes back and forth between the realms of life and art, so at times he moves toward the establishment of a "style" that is "black jade," a potentially decadent lyric-elegiac mode. In *The Dream Songs,* Berryman is fond not only of "style" as word, but of style, styles, and stylists, as question and meaning. Berryman's interest in the psychology and syntax of Shakespeare's late plays, his edition of Thomas Nashe's *The Unfortunate Traveller,* and his introduction to Matthew G. Lewis's *The Monk*[22] indicate interests of a similar kind. Unendingly, and like the other poets in this book, Berryman is aware of a defining style he needs to work out for himself, and, in the case of *The Dream Songs,* for his long poem.

The most triumphant of *The Dream Songs* manage to find that music, a style which can be austere or grand, austere and grand at the same time. The last Dream Song, no. 385, achieves a lyricism that the entire body of poems moves toward:

> My daughter's heavier. Light leaves are flying.
> Everywhere in enormous numbers turkeys will be dying
> and other birds, all their wings.
> They never greatly flew. Did they wish to?
> I should know. Off away somewhere once I knew
> such things.
>
> Or good Ralph Hodgson back then did, or does.
> The man is dead whom Eliot praised. My praise
> follows and flows too late.
> Fall is grievy, brisk. Tears behind the eyes

---

21. Pearson, "John Berryman: Poet as Medium," pp. 6-7.
22. John Berryman, Introduction to Matthew G. Lewis, *The Monk,* ed. Louis F. Peck (New York: Grove Press, 1952), pp. 11-28.

almost fall. Fall comes to us as a prize
to rouse us toward our fate.

My house is made of wood and it's made well,
unlike us. My house is older than Henry;
that's fairly old.
If there were a middleground between things and the soul
or if the sky resembled more the sea,
I wouldn't have to scold
                                        my heavy daughter.

The loving tension is maintained in the very act of the poet's
admission of some cycle which subsumes love and death.
The emotional weight of the poem and the "A Prayer for
My Daughter" tradition behind the poem keep Berryman
from the temptations of a decadent aesthetics offered along
the way. In other Dream Songs, however, the poet is not
so fortunate.

At times, love and death get on so familiarly with one
another in Berryman that the reader may forget how love
poem and memorial (day) poem, live poem and posthumous
piece blend into one. What in *The Dream Songs* first appears to be lyric frequently concludes by merging with elegy
and thus acknowledges some radical connection between
them:

The Greenhouse door was left open. Seagulls were
    screeching.
Across his face came a delicious breeze.
The gale was through.
Cat-paws of wind still ruffled the black water.
One gold line along the rubbingstrake
signalled a beauty.
                                                (No. 339)

On other occasions, elegy predominates, but so transcend-
ently as lyric elegy that the dangers may be ignored:

The leaves fall, lives fall, every little while

you can count with stirring love on a new loss
& an emptier place.
The style is black jade at all seasons, the style
is burning leaves and a shelving of moss
over each planted face.

(No. 191)

In a very basic sense, what *The Dream Songs* evidences
is an unending preparation for death or, more specifically,
for executing a death-style adequate to artful dying:

Like the breakfast bell on fire
it brings O ho it brings around again
what miserable Henry must desire:
aplomb
at the temps
of the tomb.

(No. 286)

Such desired aplomb, when achieved, would prove life style
and art style, love (poem) and death (piece) one. Or, as Berryman writes in one of the late songs, "Lilac was found
in his hand" (no. 366).

Father Hopkins said the only true literary critic is Christ.

Love & Fame, published in 1970, soon after *The Dream
Songs*, offers the same distractions and dangers of that long
work: a linguistic center which is potentially evasive, an
incipient elegiac decadence, and the sustained impression
of a posthumous, prophetic book. And it was not long before *Delusions, Etc.* and the noval *Recovery* appeared, not
as metaphorically posthumous books but as literally posthumous facts.

As with *The Dream Songs*, Berryman lends to this new
book the force of a stock-taking which becomes part of an
artistic and spiritual biography executed before a reader's
eyes. At worst, this stock-taking degenerates into another
Advertisements for Myself or another *Making It*, very much

in the American grain.

At a very basic and obvious level, Berryman attempts in *Love & Fame* to address what comes after love and after fame (which he sometimes calls "after-fame"). With the conclusion of Dream Song no. 385, Berryman announced that *The Dream Songs* were done; and in *Love & Fame* the stanzas of those songs become quatrains. Also, in the new book he seeks a unity of its own, moving more or less chronologically back to his prep school days, Columbia College, graduate school in England at "the other Cambridge," and up to his days as an established poet. But whatever differences and distance he seeks to establish in this new volume may in the end be superficial. More ghosts, technical and spiritual, linger on in *Love & Fame* than Berryman might have wanted to admit.

Love & Fame reveals familiar Berryman country. Again, there is the poet's need for caring, loving friends or "confrères"; again, the obsession with deaths and suicides of friends, writers, and fathers; again, Berryman's fears for art and love.

But time had passed since the writing and publication of *The Dream Songs,* and it is this that figures in the perspective of the book and in whatever distinctiveness and development are involved in that moving on. Even in the first two sections of *Love & Fame,* which often descend to gossip and unachieved art, Berryman writes from a new position. In *The Dream Songs,* the poet as latecomer or recent success was a prominent motif. In *Love & Fame,* Berryman is the poet who has arrived, but now he is a man even closer to mortality, more profoundly aware of his own eventual death. "I wonder if Shakespeare trotted to the jostle of his death," Berryman muses.[23] The question, however, is becoming Berryman's own in a way that it had not been for him before.

Love & Fame ostensibly moves in its last section, made

---

23. John Berryman, "Shirley & Auden," *Love & Fame* (New York: Farrar, Straus and Giroux, 1970), p. 8. Hereafter, references to poems in this volume (*L&F*) will be included in the text.

up of "Eleven Addresses to the Lord," to an art of praise,
from the love and fame recorded in the earlier sections to
a love of God the Father, in a style complexly echoic of
Donne and Herbert and Hopkins. But these addresses, concerned with praise, reveal less sureness of first and last
things than he would have liked them to.

What happens in the last section of *Love & Fame*, at least
what happens to part of Berryman as he records that part
in art, is the expression of a confessional need for a Pauline
persona or protagonist. Here is the conclusion of the last
poem of "Eleven Addresses to the Lord," with which the
book ends:

> Make too me acceptable at the end of time
> in my degree, which then Thou wilt award.
> Cancer, senility, mania,
> I pray I may be ready with my witness.

I am still not certain how much or what we are to acknowledge and accept as critic and judge. What, finally, does Berryman intend? From devotional literature, Berryman
derives the overarching metaphor for the human-divine,
love-hate drama as much as he derives the syntax (the inversion, the punning, the internal rhyming) from an earlier self
who wrote the *Sonnets* and *Homage to Mistress Bradstreet*
and *The Dream Songs*. If Berryman needs help with his
belief and unbelief, either his humility is too easy or his
language too clever to be convincing. If the puns upon "de-
gree" and "witness" are too obvious, possible puns upon
"too" (two) and "award" (a ward) — in order to reinforce
the split self which Berryman admits but wishes through
God to move beyond and to extend the judicial imagery
employed throughout — cannot easily be taken in. And the
syntax of "cancer, senility, mania," as established by the
next-to-last line, is dangerously unclear. Wit proves problematic not because it is at work against salvation (blas-
phemy, after all, as Berryman knew, could be very close
to praise), but because it seems too tired and too worn.

For a comparison with the conclusion of "Eleven Ad-

dresses to the Lord," we might look at part of an earlier
poem concluding an earlier book, 77 Dream Songs:

> these fierce & airy occupations, and love,
> raved away so many of Henry's years
> it is a wonder that, with in each hand
> one of his own mad books and all,
> ancient fires for eyes, his head full
> & his heart full, he's making ready to move on.

Dream Song no. 76, which preceded this song, is called
"Henry's Confession." And some of its confessional impulse
spills over into the adjacent poem. But confession here
favors art over religion. Whatever the amazement and
doubts and costs involved in moving on, the poet's language
on this occasion is alive enough to suggest that the loving
means and energy will be found and made available for
the necessary task. Not only has less been left to God than
in some of Berryman's later poems, but more is in evidence
because the poet chooses to stand before and sing the cre-
'ated universe and what he himself creates. What the passages
which conclude 77 Dream Songs and Love & Fame share
is the conscious figure of the poet charting territory behind
as well as future directions and intentions. The difference,
however, is that between the writing and publication of the
first book of The Dream Songs and the "Eleven Addresses
to the Lord," the concluding sequence from Love & Fame,
the confessional impulse has turned questionably volitional;
the relationship of Berryman to the reader, increasingly unsure and strained.

If anywhere at all in Love & Fame, it is in the third section
that Berryman writes poems closer to what I consider major
Berryman. These poems keep before a reader what the too
casual poems of the first two sections and which the willfully sure, tensionless poems of the last section avoid — that
horror of unlove which The Dream Songs made into a defining music. If Berryman wonders whether he might replace

the feeling of love with the more autumnal feelings of
kindness and stoical courage, he finally gives the lie to such
a dream. Here is the poem, "Despair":

> It seems to be DARK all the time.
> I have difficulty walking.
> I can remember what to say to my seminar
> but I don't know that I want to.
>
> I said in a Song once: I am unusually tired.
> I repeat that & increase it.
> I'm vomiting.
> I broke down today in the slow movement of K. 365.
>
> I certainly don't think I'll last much longer.
> I wrote: 'There may be horribles.'
> I increase that.
> (I think she took her little breasts away.)
>
> I am in love with my excellent baby.
> Crackles! in darkness HOPE; & disappears.
> Lost arts.
> Vanishings.
>
> Walt! We're downstairs,
> even you don't comfort me
> but I join your risk my dear friend & go with you.
> There are no matches
>
> Utter, His Father, one word

(L&F, 72)

Dream Song no. 28, "Snow Line," which I saw as central
to the meanings of The Dream Songs, is most prominently
behind this poem. But there are also echoes of other, partic-

ular dream songs, nos. 10, 18 ("A Strut for Roethke"), 365, and of obsessively thematic concerns running throughout that long work. Berryman reminds his reader of several kinds of dream poem: the poems about literary or — sometimes and — suicide friends and fathers; the "*Op. posth.*" poems; the poems about the fear of losing his phallus; the poems on art; the poems for his daughter. But "Despair" is in no way a simple redoing of an earlier method. Instead an earlier, manic-depressive rhythm has deepened or hardened into a more threatening and more pathetic alternation of hope and sinful despair.

Although in "Despair" it may not be dark, "it seems to be DARK all the time." And that is what is important. Behind the poem are some of the facts of Berryman's later years: the alcoholism, with its syndrome of tiredness, crying jags, vomiting, and willed forgetfulness; the pinched nerve in Berryman's foot which caused him trouble in walking; and the wish to join Whitman and the other heroic dead as well as the accompanying wish to stay and live if only some father or Father would (could?) utter some word (Word). Berryman wants matches and yet is afraid of playing with fire. "My excellent baby" at once refers to Berryman, his daughter, and Kate; the "crackles" are as likely to connect with the unwrapping of swaddling clothes as with the fireworks of apocalypse which move beyond speech and silence. Berryman ironically uses the biblical language of "increase" as he takes stock and knows how much worse a position he is in than when he wrote and lived through *The Dream Songs*. "Despair," as a poem, is controlled, incredibly so. But it records the breakdown of control in a tone that is relentlessly discriminating and exact. Berryman sets it all down: the deadly, diminutive "little breasts" whose nourishment and love seem removed from him; the placing of himself not only "downstairs" but even farther under the ground than Whitman; the realization that, in trying to add to the storehouse of the lost, vanished art of poetry, his edifice itself is in danger of autodestruction. From beginning to end, "Despair" is an extreme poetry, a poetry of high risk and cost, and most so when

Berryman understates his case by means of a parenthesis or a parenthetical "I think." Berryman knows, we know, and that is part of the pleasure and pain. For a short poem, "Despair" is one of the longest, slowest, most agonizing poems Berryman ever wrote. The other better poems in the third section of Love & Fame, which happen also to be the best poems in the book, "The Search," "Message," "Antitheses," "Of Suicide," proceed as unflinchingly as "Despair." And they comprise the poems which show the most awareness of the dramatic situation behind the book. What is there after love and fame?

Berryman was most successful and most recognizably Berryman when he was uneasy about the intimate, intricate alignments among life, fame, art, love, death, lyric, and elegy. Love & Fame is no exception. In this book, his poems still are his "lovelies." His lyrics still are, in a repeated phrase from the book, "deathwords & sayings in crisis." These are the familiar, painful connections and at times confusions or distractions which occurred in The Dream Songs. And, beyond them, is the man whom we knew through Henry as "sad a lonely." In Love & Fame, he has come to an even starker pass: "I am busy tired mad lonely & old" ("Damned," 68). Persona seems as much abandoned as Berryman seems to be playing Lear returned from storm and madness, whatever the credibility of his penetential, redemptive garments. In the face of such extremity, Berryman again knows that only love in all degrees can count, must count. In the next to last of the addresses to God which conclude Love & Fame, Berryman writes, "Father Hopkins said the only true literary critic is Christ" (95). In an interview, Berryman identified the remark as the words of Hopkins to Robert Bridges:

> Something else is in my head; a remark of Father Hopkins to Bridges. Two completely unknown poets in their thirties — fully mature — Hopkins one of the great poets of the century, and Bridges awfully good. Hopkins with no audience and Bridges with thirty readers. He says, "Fame in itself is nothing. The only thing that matters

is virtue. Jesus Christ is the only true literary critic. But,"
he said, "from any lesser level or standard than that, we
must recognize that fame is the true and appointed setting
of men of genius."[24]

But here is another context for Hopkins's remark, a letter
of Hopkins to R. W. Dixon:

> It is sad to think what disappointment must many times
> over have filled your heart for the darling children of your
> mind. Nevertheless fame whether won or lost is a thing
> which lies in the award of a random, reckless, incompe-
> tent, and unjust judge, the public, the multitude. The only
> just judge, the only just literary critic, is Christ, who
> prizes, is proud of, and admires, more than any man, more
> than the receiver himself can, the gifts of his own making.
> And the only real good which fame and another's praise
> does is to convey to us, by a channel not at all above
> suspicion but from circumstances in this case much less
> to be suspected than the channel of our own minds, some
> token of the judgment which a perfectly just, heedful,
> and wise man, namely Christ's, passes upon our doings.
> Now such a token may be conveyed as well by one as
> by many.[25]

Had Berryman also been familiar with this passage, what
connections would have interested him here? Which associations might this passage have evoked? (Also) love and
fame; the poem as love child; Hopkins's own late poem,
"Thou Art Indeed Just, Lord," as well as Hopkins's lifetime
concern with the relationship between art and religion and
with himself as poet-priest; the reception of Berryman's
own poems and books over the years.

But let us return to Berryman's line, "Father Hopkins said

24. John Berryman, "The Art of Poetry XVI: John Berryman 1914-72,"
interview by Peter A. Stitt, The Paris Review, 14, No. 53 (1972), 179-80.
    25. Gerard Manley Hopkins, letter of 13 June 1878, The Corre-
spondence of Gerard Manley Hopkins and Richard Watson Dixon, ed.
Claude Colleer Abbott (London: Oxford University Press, 1955), p. 8.

the only true literary critic is Christ." Beyond the orthodoxy
of the line, and from the larger context of the comment
by Hopkins, lies the most important connection of all. Berryman envisions the ideal figure of the critic, the critic as
Christ or as God of Love. *The Dream Songs* already had
broached such demands. With the poems in *Love & Fame,*
Berryman seeks out that same reader, but with more need
and less choice than ever before.

> *Be dust myself pretty soon; not now*
> —"Note to Wang Wei" (1958)

> *And with great good luck I'll say a little more*
> —"Dream Song No. 381" (1968)

Berryman's posthumously published work — his book of
poems, *Delusions, Etc.* and his uncompleted novel, *Recovery* — only confirm directions and dangers which I noted
in earlier volumes. We saw just how far Berryman's ironic
reserves had been depleted by the time he wrote *Love &
Fame,* when even the less cagey Henry of the late, more
direct Dream Songs seemed gone. What we witness in *Love
& Fame* is the same irony and pity which distinguished *The
Dream Songs* but with more pity and less irony than we
had seen before. In "The Home Ballad," Berryman tries to
steel himself for a return to a saner, more vigorous self,
almost in parody of the ending of a Miltonic poem also
about love and fame: "Tomorrow we'll do our best, our
best, / tomorrow we'll do our best" (*L&F,* 81). And in another poem from that volume, Berryman tries to learn and
take strength from the figure of the old woman who managed the dining room in the place where he had gone to
recover his health: "And if you can carry on so, so maybe
can I" ("Purgatory," *L&F,* 79). But on both occasions the
language rings hollow. The complexities of lyric, elegy,
blues, ballad, minstrelsy, and vaudeville dwindle to something less than art.

If in *Love & Fame* Berryman did not "entirely resign,"
he calls one of his poems in *Delusions, Etc.* "He Resigns."

If in *Love & Fame* he still saw the Blues (and, by extension, poetry as the Blues) as "the most promising mutual drama," *Recovery* descends to A. A. group therapy, which makes the possibility of recovery seem one more delusion along the way. The titles of the two posthumous books are almost beyond irony. *Delusions, Etc.* suggests in its second word the will toward some movement counter to delusion as much as it suggests pure physical, psychological, and artistic exhaustion and spiritual despair. And *Recovery* gives the lie to the emergence of recovery on every page of the book.

Both books are undistinguished. *Delusions, Etc.* has several fine poems in it, "Washington in Love," "Beethoven Triumphant," "Scholars at the Orchid Pavilion," "He Resigns," "Henry's Understanding," "Defensio in Extremis," but most of the poems are thin and artless. *Recovery* is helplessly, relentlessly bad; Berryman not only was unable to disguise his biography but unable to find the art necessary for any novel at all. Berryman falling apart — drinking himself to death, engaging in failed loving encounters, harboring incestuous desires, fouling himself behind, finding fame the last infirmity or delusion of mind — is the spectacle we never are allowed to bypass or forget. Berryman the man and writer come more and more together, ironically as Berryman comes more and more apart.

Motifs from the earlier books continue — the endless need for "the lovely men" or "unloseable friends," for love in all its forms against loss. And there is a note sounded in *Delusions, Etc.*, "We're running out / of time & fathers, sore, artless about it,"[26] which neither *The Dream Songs* nor *Love & Fame* had settled, despite the poet's attempts in the "Op. posth." poems to bury his suicide father once and for all. But I am also concerned with Berryman's word, "artless." In *Love & Fame*, he wrote "It's not my life. / That's occluded & lost" ("Message," 57). First, the life is renounced, then the art.

---

26. John Berryman, "Tampa Stomp," *Delusions, Etc.* (New York: Farrar, Straus and Giroux, 1972), p. 36.

The problem facing the critic in *Delusions, Etc.* and *Recovery*, even if he tries to forget that the books are posthumous and that Berryman finally killed himself, is that the books are full of contradictory impressions. Berryman wants to live and to die. He wants to move from lay artist to Catholic layman at the same time we wonder about his "layman's winter mockup." He wants to move to the love of the Virgin and Christ as the God of Love, while he knows that God the Father and Christ the Son have to be One. And it is easy to transpose. For "Beethoven Triumphant" read "Berryman Triumphant." For "Washington in Love" read "Berryman in Love." But the problem, as *Recovery* so chillingly sets it forth, is that the saying or hearing of "I love you" (72, 240) evokes in Berryman the most terrifying feelings of all. In part, Berryman's horror of unlove is as much Berryman's horror of love, love too good to be believed, whether in the form of love from his wife, Kate, his children, some God called the God of Love or in the form of the "killing kindness" of another writer (and close friend of Robert Lowell's), William Alfred.[27]

The poems in *Delusions, Etc.*, like the Twelve Steps of A. A. in *Recovery*, finally prove "maladaptive devices" for the poet and protagonist. If there is envy for Beethoven who was "*spared* deep age" and for those writers who did not live on into old age and so to have to say sadly, "I'm OLD" there is an accompanying willful abandonment of whatever "defenses" and "procedures" Berryman might have used as artist in the face of a continuing, aging life.

"King David Dances," the concluding poem in *Delusions, Etc.*, strikes me as a poem not of high spirits but of a desperate, pathetic strategy in the face of lovelessness and age. "All the black same I dance my blue head off!" (70). Berryman has left farther and farther behind figures like Blackface Henry, Pierrot, and Mr. Antelope.

The Dream Songs managed to suggest that there might be another method or music if only the poet could find

---

27. William Alfred, "*Orare* John Berryman," *NYRB*, 9 March 1972, p. 8.

those loving sounds. By the time of the writing of "He Resigns," however, probably the best and most significant poem in *Delusions, Etc.*, Berryman had written a poem which looked back to poems like "Snow Line" and "Despair" at the same time that it moved closer to that final dejection ode and its accompanying exhaustion which Berryman had tried so hard to stave off:

Age, and the deaths, and the ghosts.
Her having gone away
in spirit from me. Hosts
of regrets come & find me empty.

I don't feel this will change.
I don't want any thing
or person, familiar or strange.
I don't think I will sing

any more just now;
or ever. I must start
to sit with a blind brow
above an empty heart.

(D, 40)

Every word and phrase are in place; every revision and statement, carefully weighed. Yet the poem is a triumph of reductivist, minimal art precisely because lyric has shown itself to be elegy, that elegy of "black jade."

I am so happy I could scream!
It's enough! I can't BEAR ANY MORE.
Let this be it. *I've* had *it. I can't wait.*
—"The Facts & Issues" (1972)

In "Nowhere," one of the poems from *Love & Fame*, Berryman tells the lovely anecdote "of grand Unamuno setting down his profession / in the Visitors' Book on top of a Spanish mountain: / 'A humble man, & a tramp' " (21). Talking to William Meredith, Berryman had once expressed his wish to have his tombstone legend record only his name, birth and death dates, and the words, " 'Fantastic! Fantastic! Thank Thee, Dear Lord!' "[28] Whether Berryman's suicide confirms or denies that excitement and thanks proves less sure than that the posthumous books continue to show Berryman working out possible, adequate images of himself both in life and in death.

We do not need friends of Berryman's to tell us that he was "lonely" or that his "human setting was oddly thin."[29] *The Dream Songs* and the books that followed are full of those facts. More complex are some of the connections and parallels which Berryman made in his lifetime between his own life and eventual death and the lives and deaths of other writers, especially poets, and poets like Dylan Thomas, Jarrell, Schwartz, and Plath. Although Sylvia Plath killed herself almost ten years before Berryman killed himself, she is the one figure who draws herself or who is drawn by Berryman into some orbit of inevitability and sorrow. Here is Saul Bellow writing of Berryman's end:

> And at last it must have seemed that he had used up all his resources. Faith against despair, love versus nihilism had been the themes of his struggles and his poems. What he needed for his art had been supplied by his own person, by his mind, his wit. He drew it out of his vital organs, out of his very skin. At last there was no more. Reinforcements failed to arrive. Forces were not joined. The cycle of resolution, reform and relapse had become a bad joke which could not continue.
>
> (Foreword, *R*, xiv)

Behind the passage, whether consciously or unconsciously, is the account of A. Alvarez of Sylvia Plath's last days, when help also failed to arrive by that chain of accidents,

---

28. William Meredith, "In Loving Memory of the Late Author of *The Dream Songs*," *The Virginia Quarterly Review*, 49 (1973), 73.
29. Saul Bellow, Foreword to Berryman, *Recovery*, p. xiv.

mistakes, or coincidences which Alvarez describes[30] and in conjunction with probably the worst London winter in 150 years, when "the gas failed and Sunday joints were raw. The lights failed and candles, of course, were unobtainable. Nerves failed and marriages crumbled. Finally, the heart failed. It seemed the cold would never end. Nag, nag, nag."[31]

What happened to Plath's resources and to Berryman's resources at the conclusion of their lives was apparent, however, not only to Bellow after the fact of the second death but to Berryman during his own life. Her life and end held the kind of resonance for him which only his own suicide could fully own. Like Plath, Berryman poses for us some of the same questions about whether the death and art were worth what the life and art could or could not contain.

In one of the finest attempts to deal with what had happened by the time Berryman was writing the novel *Recovery*, David Kalstone has written:

> For Berryman the new and harrowing departure must have been the almost impossible demand that exposure, truth about the self, might even be divorced from "literary merit." That had been, after all, the secret strength of Henry Pussycat in the "Dream Songs," the resourcefulness with which vulnerability leapt to power, flirted with danger, kept its skeleton, Mr. Bones, charmingly by its side. That very resourcefulness is the enemy of "Recovery," just as the copious dark renewals of almost 400 Dream Songs would be a threat to the merciless candor of the Twelve Steps.[32]

Kalstone presents his speculations and judgment in an argument which never descends to a suggestion that Berryman, like so many minor confessional artists, simply could not

---

30. A. Alvarez, "Prologue: Sylvia Plath," *The Savage God: a Study of Suicide* (London: Weidenfeld and Nicolson, 1971), pp. 28-31.

31. Ibid., p. 28.

32. David Kalstone, review of *Recovery, The New York Times Book Review*, 27 May 1973, p. 3.

afford to get well. Yet the questions raised are not unrelated
to those which modern confessional literature continually
is forced to deal in. That Berryman's strategies are thrown
into question, I would agree, but Berryman himself had
been aware of this way back in *The Dream Songs* themselves.

As Berryman sought out in his two posthumous books
what his delusions were — and the word not only runs
throughout them both but emerges as a revisionist impulse
in the interview done by Peter Stitt which Berryman went
back to and corrected with footnotes ("Get the delusion"
or the repeated "Delusion")[33] — he came to show just how
"slow" a "burn" and how great a "thirst" and "hunger"
The Dream Songs gave and made. Whether Berryman's suicide and posthumously published work show him "fending
off torrents of a grace that has become unbearable,"[34] we
may question or share as interpretation. But in the increasing evidence which *Delusions, Etc.* and *Recovery* bring to
Berryman's horror of unlove, perhaps even horror of love
as I suggested earlier, one thing emerges as uncontroverti-
ble. We come to know just how profoundly ambiguous a
law against Henry and against Berryman there is.

---

33. Berryman, "The Art of Poetry XVI," *passim.*
34. Meredith, "In Loving Memory of the Late Author of *The Dream
Songs*," p. 78.

Chapter Three

Robert Creeley: "Locate *I* / *Love* You"

The critic's constant intentions to the things he discussed
directed, after all, such ways of speaking as: for, with
and about

—Louis Zukofsky

Writing as far back as 1960, Robert Creeley found things
"pinched emotionally, pinched referentially — despite the
fact that the moon comes closer."[1] In response to that
evaluation of the time and world in which he knows himself
to be living, Creeley has thrown the entire weight of his
poetic corpus upon the primacy of the poetic act and fact
(poem). The direction in his verse from his earliest poems
to the recent unpaginated *A Day Book*, has been to move
back (in time) and down (in mind) to a level where thinking
and feeling have their very source. Repeatedly, as the poem
"Variations" indicates, Creeley is engaged in that ritual
drama and dance where *"these senses recreate"* all that is

---

1. Robert Creeley, "Olson & Others: Some Orts for the Sports." *A
Quick Graph: Collected Notes & Essays*, ed. Donald Allen (San Francisco: Four Seasons Foundation, 1970), p. 166

and was and will be, both word and world.[2]

If the basic making of poems proves to be focus and intention, the danger for Creeley is that of resisting and surviving the moon's greater proximity and all other learning and intelligence which seek to undo him every day and night of his life. It is no wonder, then, that so many of his poems address root questions of being: thinking, knowing, doing, and saying. For Creeley, these are all matters of the most intense feeling. As the last poem of Creeley's book, *Pieces,* concludes:

What do you do,
what do you say,
what do you think,
what do you know.[3]

Out of context, the lines sound almost trite. But in context and because of the absence of quotation marks these lines mark one of the very moving extremities of Creeley's art.

The process of thinking occupies so major a part of Creeley's poetry that it is easy for misunderstandings to arise. Creeley can be abstract, metaphysical. But his thinking concurrently engages problems of feeling wherever it proceeds and whatever it touches. For Creeley, thinking is as radically dramatic and emotive as in plays which typify the modern drama. August Strindberg's "cerebral marriage" and "cerebral child" in *The Father,* Luigi Pirandello's " 'cerebral drama' " in *Six Characters in Search of an Author,* and Edward Albee's "mental sex play" in *Tiny Alice* come close to the radical cerebralism prominent in Creeley's verse.[4]

---

2. Robert Creeley, "Variations," *Words* (New York: Charles Scribner's Sons, 1967), p. 42. Hereafter, references to poems in this volume (*W*) will be included in the text.

3. Robert Creeley, "When he and I," *Pieces* (New York: Charles Scribner's Sons, 1969), p. 81. Hereafter, references to poems in this volume (*P*) will be included in the text.

4. August Strindberg, *The Father,* trans. Elizabeth Sprigge, *Six Plays of Strindberg* (New York: Doubleday & Company, 1955), p. 55; Luigi

As a poet, Creeley not only acknowledges poetry as his metier but language as the medium through which his thinking occurs and is shaped:

You want

the fact

of things

in words,

of words.

("Like a man committed," P, 61)

However much Creeley admits the importance of pause, silence, and the nonverbal arts, he returns to thinking in words as the way of ordering his world. Events, people, things, gestures, and relationships give the impression of being minutely, scrupulously re-created by Creeley, as if their sole reality depended upon the poet's thinking them out in verse. At times, Creeley threatens to rival the intensities of a Monsieur Teste or of a protagonist in a Beckett novel.

Creeley occasionally expresses a disgust at the need to think. "Agh — man / thinks," he writes (P, 69). But in reading Creeley, as in reading Williams, we must and can distinguish between thinking as a limited, analytic activity and as some more elemental process which involves feeling of the most intense kind. Thinking in words becomes for Creeley an effort which can assume the proportions of a godlike remaking of a world.

In both his poetry and his prose, Creeley's lifetime devotion has been to return language not to some naive primitivism but to a situation where language and, in turn, thinking

Pirandello, Six Characters in Search of an Author, trans. Edward Storer, Naked Masks, ed. Eric Bentley (New York: E. P. Dutton & Co., 1958), p. 258; Edward Albee, Tiny Alice (New York: Atheneum, 1965), pp. 112-13.

and feeling, could be purer and more exact. Sharing the wishful concern of older modernists for a redeeming language, Creeley's verse is full of a hatred of cliché and cant. Talking in 1965 about some of the participants at a poetry conference at Berkeley which he attended, Creeley turned with excitement to the possibility of returning words "to an almost primal circumstance ... to an almost objective state of presence so that *they* speak rather than someone speaking with them."[5] Behind such intentions stand figures like Pound and Williams, as much as younger but by now middle-aged poets like Gary Snyder and Creeley himself.

Creeley's own poetry is never far from these root concerns of realigning word and world. Words and things may never be one, particularly for a culture as literary as the Anglo-American tradition continues to be. But some of the polarization that has occurred between language and particulars can be bridged. Creeley's poetry recurrently addresses itself to this responsibility and action.

Creeley goes back not just to the origins of poetic creation but to the basics of using any language at all. What intrigues and obsesses him is man as word-maker and tool-user. His poems are replete with the activities of naming and numbering, of declining and conjugating the various parts of speech. Person, case, mood, and tense are legitimate and vital concerns. Creeley must be grammarian and syntactician in order to make poetry again possible in some fundamental sense:

> He / I
> were walking. Then
> the place *is / was*
> not ever enough.

                                        ("A Sight," W, 101)

Such moments prove representative, painfully typical in fact. They are part of an unending examination by the poet of every available and existent idiom. Phrases like "enough

---

5. Robert Creeley, "An Interview with Robert Creeley, 1965," interview by Linda Welshimer Wagner, *The Minnesota Review*, 5 (1965), 310.

is enough" prove to be statement and cliché as well as an
index to the reverse of what Creeley knows, that enough
is never enough. The ending of Creeley's poem, "Enough,"
oddly suggests by its syntax and repetitions the opposite
of what it says: "I vow to yours to be / enough, enough,
enough" (W, 127). A similar procedure is evident in his
endless quotation marks around overused words and ex-
pressions we are daily surrounded with.

Creeley is determined to search out every possible pun.
His single, physical eye ("I") — photographs of him provide
an entire series of studies of their own in this regard —
terrifyingly takes him to the ground-base of seeing, saying,
and knowing. It is a procedure that is relentless and eternal.
In turn, metaphor and simile, instead of being useful for
the poet, plague Creeley for the evasive devices they can
become:

> Mississippi much as — pen blots
> with pressure (?) — the sky ahead
> a faint light yellow — like "northern"
> lights. — Why the goddamn impatience
> with that AS — the damn function of
> *simile,* always a displacement of
> what *is* happening.
>
> ("Forms' passage," P, 49)

> I hate the metaphors.
> I want you. I am still alone,
> but want you with me.
>
> ("Could write of fucking–," P, 76)

At worst, imagistic language threatens to conceal the very
possibilities it was meant to illuminate. Against these temptations, Creeley stresses the need not only for a more careful
handling of language but of matters as basic as breath and
syllable.

Creeley also uncovers a preference for a basic poetics
in his attention to the importance of etymology and of parts
of speech often considered to be at best minor: prepositions,

articles, and conjunctions.

"Throw," "throw up," and "throw together" provide Creeley with the kind of serious playfulness that etymology can offer the poet:

So will
words throw (throw up) their meaning.[6]

[Creeley is writing on Olson's poetics in his Introduction to Olson's *Selected Writings 2*]

In *Mayan Letters* we have unequivocal evidence of a *kind* of intelligence which cannot propose the assumption of content prior to its experience of that content, which *looks,* out of its *own* eyes. This does not mean that conjecture is to be absent, insofar as *jacio* means "throw" and *con,* "together" — however simply this may note the actual process.[7]

When Creeley addresses himself to how words "throw up" their meaning, we are also reminded of the very violence of the creative act — taking us back to literary and pictorial representations of the mythological Sibyl, foaming at the mouth and writhing on the floor during a visionary seizure.

Prepositions, conjunctions, and articles matter to Creeley as much as the linguistic stores of etymology. Prepositions and the nuances they allow are as strategic to Creeley as to poets as distant in time and different as Emily Dickinson and Louis Zukofsy. In the title of his first major collection, *For Love,* Creeley's choice and use of a preposition indicated a preference and direction which continue throughout all of his work and which this chapter will seek to bear out.

Creeley also deals radically with conjunctions. One of his poems, "For W. C. W.," assigns to *"and"* the force of a

6. Robert Creeley, "The Epic Expands," *The Charm: Early and Uncollected Poems* (San Francisco: Four Seasons Foundation, 1969), p. 17. Hereafter, references to poems in this volume (*TC*) will be included in the text.

7. Robert Creeley, "Introduction to Charles Olson: *Selected Writings 2,*" *A Quick Graph,* p. 182.

newly discovered word intimately connected with the Adamic prerogatives of creation:

> There, you say, and
> there, and there,
> and *and* becomes
>
> just so.
>
> (W, 27)

The definite and indefinite articles, "the," "a," "an," occur in Creeley's verse as part of a similar clearing, cleansing process. There is the sense that they, too, proceeded from a poetics that could afford to take nothing for granted. When Creeley delineates "a" and "the," a drama ensues of the most intense, intent kind.

The drama which Creeley can uncover in the use of articles, definite and indefinite, provides a way for him to underline extreme tensions. Without such devices, Creeley might have lacked a language adequate to the exactions of such crises in feeling and thought. A poem like "The Window" makes this unmistakable. Behind Creeley's sense of the advantages to which articles, as more than just parts of speech, might be put, is the figure of Zukofsky, the poet whose long poem is entitled "A." In an impassioned prose piece, Zukofsky wrote:

> The poet wonders why so many today have raised up the word "myth," finding the lack of so-called "myths" in our time a crisis the poet must overcome or die from, as it were, having become too radioactive, when instead a case can be made out for the poet giving some of his life to the use of the words *the* and *a:* both of which are weighted with as much epos and historical destiny as one man can perhaps resolve. Those who do not believe

this are too sure the little words mean nothing among
so many other words.[8]

Not only has Creeley in his prose acknowledged Zukofsky
as a poet and poet-critic of great importance, but he has
dedicated individual poems and an entire volume of poems
called *Pieces* to him. Creeley's own manner of using articles
in his poetry approaches the mythical, mystical dimension
Zukofsky attends to in this selection.

In Creeley primacy involves not only articles, conjunctions, and prepositions. It also figures in Creeley's attention
to a "basic place to live."[9] It is not accidental that Creeley
has spent so much time living in the elemental parts of New
England, New Mexico, and Spain.

This primacy extends, too, to his themes and to the poet's
unending wrestle with the problem of form and content
("Form is never more than an extension of content").[10] The
themes which Creeley has engaged in his prose writings
on poetry include those with which poetry has commonly
dealt: war, love between man and woman, friendship, and
the land. Creeley cited Olson for the particular formulation
and awareness of these motifs in Olson's own work.[11]
But Creeley might have gone to any number of other poets
in this or some earlier century for what is finally support
and confirmation rather than source.

What links these themes is love. In this light, war is a
perversion of love; friendship, a kind of love between men,
between women, and between men and women; and land
is the occasion for a relationship involving care and love
or their reverse.

Not only are these themes basic but so are the people

---

8. Louis Zukofsky, "Poetry," *Prepositions: The Collected Critical
Essays of Louis Zukofsky* (London: Rapp & Carroll Ltd., 1967), p. 18.
9. Robert Creeley, "The Art of Poetry X: Robert Creeley," interview
by Linda Wagner and Lewis MacAdams, Jr., *The Paris Review*, 11, No.
44 (1968), 179.
10. Creeley, "An Interview with Robert Creeley, 1965," p. 317.
11. Creeley, "The Art of Poetry X: Robert Creeley," pp. 180-81; Creeley, "An Interview with Robert Creeley, 1965," p. 312.

necessarily involved in them. If we look at the poems too
rapidly, Creeley may appear to be indulging in the abstract.
In fact, Creeley deals with men and women repeatedly in
ways that are radically archetypal. As he writes in a poem
for his daughter:

There will not be another
woman such as you
are. Remember
your mother,

the way you came,
the days of waiting.
Be natural,
daughter, wise

as you can be,
all my daughters,
be women
for men

when that time comes.[12]

This poem, in a tradition of occasional poems for daughters,
manages to be so basic that it risks abstraction. And it does
this in the very act of moving toward consideration of the
fullest particularity available to the daughter as a woman.

A post-Nietzschean, post-Freudian humor and sophistica-
tion in other Creeley poems present similar dangers. By
such a stance, Creeley threatens to displace the radical relationships involved. Some of the longer poems in *Words*
especially underscore the unending sexual dramas going on
in Creeley's work at the deepest levels. These levels acknowledge the figures of Oedipus and Onan, as much as
they show the kind of paraliterary concerns in which criti-

---

12. Robert Creeley, "The Name," *For Love: Poems 1950-1960* (New
York: Charles Scribner's Sons, 1962), pp. 144-45. Hereafter, references
to poems in this volume (*FL*) will be included in the text.

cism of a poet like Creeley increasingly may be forced to deal. Not only is Creeley's "I" heavy upon him and upon us as readers, but that "I" keeps opening out to painfully, playfully address the most basic wishes or guilts and fears of all women and all men. The ground is not only abstractly metaphysical but intently personal. In poems like "The Woman," "The Dream," and "A Sight," Creeley manages to give us some sense of the real, particular contexts to which his dreams attach.

The titles of numerous Creeley poems underline how basic are the figures who people and take part in the dramas and relationships the poems record: "The Boy," "The Friend," "All That Is Lovely in Men," "I Know a Man," "The Woman," "The Wife," "Kids Walking," "Citizen," "The Family." Again, instead of instancing abstraction, these titles show how Creeley relentlessly returns only to central — human, domestic, loving — things.

> The imagination may be compared to Adam's dream —
> he awoke and found it truth
> > > —John Keats

> O lovely cherry tree, come true.
> Together we could celebrate the years.
> > —Hugo Williams, "Cherry Blossom"

Human and loving considerations never are very far from Creeley, and from the beginning he has sought to make his work into "this / garden of particular / intent" ("The Question," TC, 35). The matter is one of agreement and arrangement, "the fashion of a stone / underground" ("A Poem," TC, 36). What concern him are mystery and love, relationships carried and contained: between words and page, reader and poem, poetry and prose, language and world. It is a poem-by-poem possibility as much as it is the day-to-day possibility that prose — novel, short story, lyric prose like "A Day Book" — allows. These possibilities connect, in turn, with one of the radical impulses of lyric, to make self, tree, and world come true:

I want to grow in ground too,
want it to come true
what they said about if you planted
the acorn the tree would grow.

                              ("The Kid," *FL*, 112)

Wish I were an apple seed
and had John what's-his-name
to plant me.[13]

In nonfictional prose, Creeley also has attested to this American, Adamic undertaking:

In poems I have both discovered and born testament to
my life in ways no other possibility has given me. Can
I *like* all that I may prove to be, or does it matter? Am
I merely living for my own approval? In writing it has
seemed to me that such small senses of existence were
altogether gone, and that, at last, the world "came true."[14]

Yet the possibility or variability which Creeley finds so attractive in poetry and the "small senses of existence" which
he finds gone when he is within that art sometimes desert
the simple boundaries assigned to them here.

What Creeley wants and needs to be real or true frequently concludes by not staying real or by turning untrue. A
recurrent fear of his is that of finding the empty pool of
Eliot as final fact:

Nothing says anything
but that which it wishes
would come true, fears
what else might happen in

---

13. Robert Creeley, *A Day Book* (New York: Charles Scribner's Sons,
1972), n. p. Hereafter, references to poems in this volume will be included
in the text; because of the lack of pagination, no page numbers can
be given.
14. Robert Creeley, "I'm given to write poems," *A Quick Graph*, p.
72.

some other place, some
other time not this one
A voice in my place, an
echo of that only in yours.

("For Love," *FL*, 160)

So tenuous is the balance that the poet wishes and fears
within a particular movement that it becomes a feat of both
the emotional and the artistic life. The dichotomies —
"wishes"/"fears," "nothing"/"anything," "other"/"this,"
"my"/"yours" — meticulously reflect how much is at stake.

Creeley's fears engage many things. Sometimes he fears
a false volitionalism, either in his own poetry or in the work
of others. He knows how, at best, words create their own
world, how "*and* becomes/just so." He also knows how
the process of willing poetry into being not only assures
nothing but may not be enough:

[On Anthony Ostroff's *Imperatives*]
The technical means seem competent, although stiffly
present — again, the will "to write" "a poem" is dominant.
And the intelligence is so battered in the process of getting
it all, just so, together, that very little else otherwise gets
said.

[On Brother Antoninus's *The Hazards of Holiness*]
But I cannot avoid nor deny the force of this language,
despite my own characterization of it as often melodra-
matic, that is, an enlargement of occasion purely willed.[15]

Creeley's discriminating criticism of these other poets' work
in part is made possible by what he learned from Abstract
Expressionism and Action Painting, two arts of infinite gra-
dation where one false line can obliterate everything in-
stantly.

---

15. Robert Creeley, " 'Think what's got away . . .,' " *A Quick Graph*,
pp. 264-65, 262.

Creeley's fears about the falsely volitional indicate how trustworthy and untrustworthy words can be at the same time. "Words" are "full / of holes / aching" ("The Language," *W*, 37), waiting, wanting to be filled and made whole. This is the simplicity of the situation, variously recorded throughout Creeley's work. But it is never simple for Creeley to act on or for us to watch Creeley re-create. There are moments in Creeley when volitional successes reach toward a graceful sufficiency or natural ease, as in the release and pleasure afforded by these couplets or quasi couplets:

Enough for now to be here, and
To know my door is one of these.

("Return," *TC*, 3)

What in the light's form finds her face,
makes of her eyes the simple grace.

("The Fire," *W*, 29)

This life cannot be lived
apart from what it must forgive.

("Flowers," *P*, 5)

These moments, while taken from different Creeley books written over a period of years, are rare for the poet who, as a Puritan, often can only "think of everything / as earned" ("For Love," *FL*, 159).

Creeley has so much difficulty accepting anything that is unearned that he turns his poetry into a stocktaking which will help compensate for whatever inadequacy or unavailability seems to threaten all the time. Warren Tallman, in writing about Creeley's short stories, has observed:

In "A Death" children play with sticks and throw stones and the sticks recur as twigs, trees, the chairs mentioned, as boats, as tables, and the stones recur as pebbles, as rocks, boulders, gravestones, chunks of gold.
In one real sense these sticks and stones and their

variants are both elementary and elemental in Creeley's world, as elementary as the childhood nursery saw and as elemental to his spaces as rock and wood are to the actual world. They stand about in his tales in much the way that Klee's arrows or Chagall's violins stand about in their paintings.[16]

Tallman's comparisons are of a telling kind. What they neglect to acknowledge, however, is a less comforting strategy in Creeley's work, also dreamlike but involved with a more desperate, pathetic attempt to have or keep anything at all.

"Words, words / as if all / worlds were there," Creeley wrote in his poem, "A Token" (FL, 123). What we know is that all worlds are not there, however much Creeley would like, in some moments at least, to bridge the gap between word and world. Here is Creeley concluding his preface to For Love:

> In any case, we live as we can, each day another — there is no use in counting. Nor more, say, to live than what there is, to live. I want the poem as close to this fact as I can bring it; or it, me.
>
> (7)

The intention is clear, but the satisfaction of that wish, like Creeley's wish to write poems in behalf of love, often runs into oppositional difficulties.

The nature of language fascinates and arouses Creeley as often as it makes him despair. As verbal medium, it is approximate. Yet, because of this, it refuses to stop reminding him of its human context and use.

At worst, words tend to falsify or get in between the experience they are to record. By the time the words are said, they seem beyond the occasion the poet needed them for:

---

16. Warren Tallman, "Robert Creeley's Portrait of the Artist," *Three Essays on Creeley* (Toronto: The Coach House Press, 1973), n. p.

Late, the words, late
the form of them, al-
ready past what they were
fit for, one and two and three.

("Place," *P,* 43)

By the time things have occurred, their occurrence is nonre-
peatable, and their relationship is threatened by a stubborn
discreteness. "One and two and three" pass away, forever,
one, two, three. But in the face of this situation the poet
is never idle. The poet becomes an historian; and the historian, approximating R. G. Collingwood's ideal sense of him,
becomes an artist. Creeley offers "the activity of writing"
as his conception of writing; and, "the activity of evidence,"
as his conception of history.[17] What counts is the artistry
of the activity. As Creeley moves toward a consideration
of what the poet can do with and within language, possibility and variability return to him in order to show how necessity can be freedom:

It is very possible that what one defines, as means, as
possibilities, will prove only a temporary instance, a place
soon effaced by other use, as when a whole city block
is leveled to make a parking lot, or park. But that is the
risk. One cannot avoid it, or do otherwise.[18]

The larger processes of displacement and effacement, instead of creating despair, also can signal renewal of the
most radical kind. Or, to alter the terms slightly, what had
seemed the fated imperative of endless want and dissatis-
faction can provide its own countermovement toward language and love:

It isn't that one wants what one gets, or doesn't. One

---

17. Creeley, "Introduction to Charles Olson: *Selected Writings 2,*" *A
Quick Graph,* p. 188.
18. Creeley, "Why Bother?" *A Quick Graph,* p. 41.

wants it, gets it, doesn't want it, does, gets it again. It
is endless . . . He touched her. One does it over and over,
as he did. The tree is no different, the sun is no different.
It comes again.[19]

That "it comes again" is a comforting fact, but only partially. For "it" refers as much to need which reasserts itself
endlessly as to the satisfaction of desire. The words have
to be written out, over and over; and love, made again and
again. Creeley's stated attraction to Blake's poem, "The
Question Answered," may be illuminating in this regard:

> What is it men in women do require?
> The lineaments of gratified desire.
> What is it women do in men require?
> The lineaments of gratified desire.[20]

The rhyming of "require" and "desire" points to a volitional
merging of sound and sense. But the riddling center of the
poem and the tension which is set up between "lineaments"
and "gratified desire" suggest how great a gap may exist
between the two full-rhyme words, for Creeley if not for
Blake. In Creeley's own poetry, it is the rhyming of "insistent" or "persistent" with "resistant" which provides the
best example of how provisional word and world finally
are. If poetry makes things come true, Creeley confronts
the continuing danger that poetry may unsay and deny its
linguistic relationship with the larger concerns of locating
love and self.

The supreme consciousness with which Creeley imposes
upon us his intentional strategies — to write on behalf of
or for love, to make language come true, and to align language with matters of love and self — creates difficulty precisely because of the desperateness of the strategies involved. That the maneuvers are desperate Creeley frequent-

---

19. Robert Creeley, *The Island* (New York: Charles Scribner's Sons,
1963), pp. 33, 43.
20. Quoted (actually slightly misquoted) by Creeley in "A Note,"
A Quick Graph, p. 345.

ly succeeds in making us forget, as in the concluding
lyricism of the last story in The Gold Diggers:

> Get the book to her. Get the goddamn book to her. Show
> her what you can do. The book with the songs.[21]

Since "goddamn" is part of the celebratory, assertive
rhythms of the tale, it tends to conceal possibilities for
darker interpretations. Elsewhere, however, Creeley's loving strategies present vexing confusions and contradictions
for the critic. The endless procedure of writing or saying
love, which I pointed to earlier in Creeley, is centrally involved. But even more telling are those moments when
Creeley wonders why he writes at all and when he expresses the need to write, that "insistence of his own existence,"[22] in grudging, understated terms. Here are two such
moments, one from his poetry and one from his short
stories:

> It still makes sense
> to know the song after all.
>
> ("The Song," FL, 117)

> Sometime you will have to answer me, she said. Some-
> time there will be nothing else for you to do.[23]

The tone, from its assertive to sad ranges, lingers hauntingly
long after the books in which these admissions appear are
put away. Creeley's announced poetic strategies for finding
love and self prove less sure the more we look at the work.
To see briefly what Creeley has been doing as a developing
poet may help clarify some of the discrepancies I have been
intimating up to this point.

Creeley's four major books, For Love, Words, Pieces, A
Day Book, all attend in their titles to language, however

---

21. Robert Creeley, "The Book," The Gold Diggers and Other Stories
(New York: Charles Scribner's Sons, 1965), p. 158.
22. Creeley, "An Interview with Robert Creeley, 1965," p. 312.
23. Robert Creeley, "The Party," The Gold Diggers, p. 57.

differently each book expresses preferences for anything
from short, formal love lyric to fragmented, open or dense
prose. Although *Pieces* less consistently yields the pleasures
and satisfactions of the other three works, I see it as a book
which Creeley had to write. What I am interested in now
is the continuing tensions which inform all four of the books
and how much Creeley has changed from collection to collection.

For Love announced in its title Creeley's intentional strategy. And Creeley's *Words* later underlined some intimate
connection between words and love. More important is
what Creeley exposes as working against offering love
poems or a love book. We encounter in *For Love* not just
cruelty and indifference but gratuitous cruelty and intentional indifference. And feelings of pettiness, petulance, dis-
trust, anger, hate, silence. Such emotions need not be divorced from love. Sometimes ugly emotions, when
re-examined by Creeley in *For Love,* allow him to move
back to the emotions which he wants the book to be for:
"into the company of love / it all returns" (160), he concludes the last and title poem of the book. But too many
of the other poems record a resistant self, a metaphysical
amorist afraid and unable to love, a poet-lover most brilliant
in the acknowledgement of love which has become unlove,
a perversion and perversity of will.

Words only deepens such impressions in the very act of
seeking, like *For Love,* to exist as a book written in behalf
of love. Words, love, and self have to be insisted upon too
often:

when was something to

happen, had I secured
that — had I, *had*
I, insistent.

                              ("Some Place," *W,* 77)

What am I to myself
that must be remembered

insisted upon
so often?

("The Rain," FL, 109)

Creeley's "measure / resistant" proves either that insistence
is not enough or that there are threats to the creation of
a loving self which come as gothic dislocations of perspective or as intrusive diminutives of fact:

Hoo, hoo —
laughter.

Hoo, hoo —
laughter.

Obscene
distance.

("Enough," W, 124-25)

        and under his
feet the rug bunches.

("One Way," W, 59)

        So little love
to share among so many.

("The Messengers," W, 31)

Even more resistant to the establishment of Words as a love
book is the gratuitous cruelty, familiar to us from parts of
For Love and courted by the poet:

We break things in pieces like
walls we break ourselves into
hearing them fall just to hear it.

("The Answer," W, 82)

Or, to be kinder and fairer to Creeley, it may be the at-once
personal and universal depiction of life as surreal, real pain
in Words which threatens every instance of love:

Pieces

I didn't
want
to hurt you.
Don't

stop
to think It
hurts,
to live

like this,
meat
sliced
walking.

(W, 104)

If there is any way out of such a situation, some of the
poems in Words hint that it will have to come in the form
of a new sensibility of poetics where older, easy unities
of self or of pairings come apart. "Pieces" was the title of
one of the poems in Words, and we have looked at that
poem. It proved so important as direction and impulse that
Creeley chose it for the title of his next major book.

Like For Love and Words, Pieces ostensibly seeks a poetics of self, through love. "As I love / My poetics," Zukofsky
wrote.[24] But what we see happening in Pieces, as in the
earlier books of Creeley, is that these equations or associations prove not as simple as the poet would make them
appear. For Love and Words presented much that was "resistant" to love, yet we encounter in those books nothing
as radical as what surfaces in Pieces. At worst, we get either
a poetry of exhaustion or entropy — "So tired / it falls /
apart" (P, 48) — or, even more dangerous, the debasement

---

24. Louis Zukofsky, "A"-12, "A" 1-12 (New York: Doubleday& Company, Inc., 1967), p. 157.

of love into a sentimental gospel of a latter-day beat community:

    and two by two
    is not an army
    but friends who love

    one another.

                            ("Numbers," P, 25)

Throughout *Pieces*, always in search of some kind of loving oneness, Creeley keeps trying to come together or break apart.

    Pieces is full of the same paradoxes and holes which marked the earlier books. *For Love and Words* sought to create an ark where men and women could walk "two by two." Yet, what continually threatened the poet in those books was the impasse of "one." Instead of the mystical one, or the mathematical-sexual one ("one over one"), what ensued was that "one" separated from self and from love. This also proves to be the case in the numbering procedures which mark the poems in *Pieces*:

    All this dances in a room,
    two by two, but alone.

                            ("Gemini," P, 15)

    One, two,
    is the rule —

    from there to three
    simple enough.

    Now four
    makes the door

    back again
    to one and one.

                            ("Some Nights," P, 74)

The substance of one
is not two. No thought
can ever come to that.

("Such strangeness of mind," *P,* 79)

Even more extremely, at the center of any number or nu-
merical, geometrical form, Creeley always discovers pain
or struggle:

Oct-
ag-
on-
al.

("Numbers," *P,* 31)

Fragmented, but still at the center, is the Greek word *agon.*
Similarly, when Creeley picks a flower, the petals, plucked
one by one, become emblems only of struggle and pain.
In his poem from *For Love* called "The Business," love had
been "a remote chance on / which you stake / yourself"
(44). Again, pain was prominent, yet the pun and line division indicated other possibilities, even if martyred ones, for
self and love.

Creeley occasionally shifts the existence of pain as a recurrent fact in *Pieces* into more playful terms which can
address fear and change and death as things which attest
to a world that is sad, lovely, and weird at the same time:

You are all lovely,
hairy, scarey
people after all.

("Situation of feeling," *P,* 53)

        So
much has gone
away.

("Ice Cream," *P,* 56)

If not grace notes, these were notes also sounded in books

of poems that appeared before *Pieces.*

But if there is some important continuity with this book and the earlier ones, it is to its position as a book of breakthrough and breakdown and to its particular recordings of the intricacies of loving feeling that I wish to return. Creeley the Puritan is as much in evidence in this book as those that went before. But the unfinished, raw feel of much of the book I find due less to some Puritan aesthetic of God's altar not needing Creeley's polishing as to some muddy, muddled aesthetic handed down, whether directly or deviously from the beats. What is not secondhand, although it again suggests parallels with an earlier beat consciousness, is Creeley's insistent wish not to be "up tight" (as he put it), not to be the lone, lonely Puritan.

Throughout *Pieces* Creeley ventures that the way out of the limitations of his "ego structure" must involve finding and merging with some Muse or White Goddess figure, variously Athena, Circe, Minerva, Diana, *la belle dame sans merci,* forest princess, wife. At other times, he ventures that the way out is the way back to the womb or breast where (when) the foetus or child was still one with the mother; or that the way out is the recovery of the other half whose division from the self Aristophanes explains in Plato's *Symposium* as the origin of the sexes. But in all cases what mediates against such "lovely" union proves the "lonely" isolation of "one."

Just how much the location of self through love involves the complex paradoxes of two-as-one and one-as-two Creeley never lets us forget; near the end of *Pieces* he is still with what he would like to escape from:

Why one, why two,
why not go utterly
away from all of it.

("Such strangeness of mind," P, 80)

On this occasion, Creeley's desperate wish constitutes getting away not only from singles and singleness but from

doubles which occasionally provided him with comfort
elsewhere in *Pieces*. The wish to "go utterly / away from
all of it" casts a shadow across earlier moments either of
mystical harmony or comic sanity:

> and all the bodies together
> are, one by one, the measure.
>
> ("Why say," *P*, 49)

> Love one.
> Kiss two.
>
> ("The day comes and goes," *P*, 66)

And, when, near the end of the book he redoes as "Four"
the section on that number in "Numbers," "a secure / fact
of things" or "love's triumph" which that number once
brought him is replaced by:

> Before I die.
> Before I die.
> Before I die.
> Before I die.
>
> (*P*, 71)

What *Pieces* seems to say as it goes on to its conclusion,
becoming a long poem made up of quick takes, word games,
formal lyrics, dirty jokes, bits of conversation, is that, if
"the power to tell / is glory" ("The Finger," *P*, 10), it is a
poor power that has to be asserted and insisted upon, like
that of self and love, endlessly:

> Again
> and again
> now
> also.
>
> ("I cannot see you," *P*, 14)

The insistence stands in the face of change and mortality,
when one is most oneself, Creeley seems to say, seconding

Freud. Here, and elsewhere in *Pieces*, the poet suggests that if primitive systems returned to "one" with the satisfaction of familiarity and recurrence, this is not the case for him. More often than not, "one" suggests the isolate, lonely, relentless fact of the moon shining on, the wife next to but separate from him in bed, the poet separate from some potentially truer self. *Pieces* becomes an enormous effort to muster enough "will" to become "one" with another person or simply to trustingly "follow" what that other promises as union. But Creeley knows that "will," an image of mind, risks, as in his poem "The Finger," creating not love but a finger-fuck. And he knows that to "follow" can mean to find himself in Circe's bed. Beyond these problems, is the question of whether he and we can ever know another person or "one" at all.

Bobbie's Law

"Every one
having the two."

A Day Book continues and complicates what all of Creeley's books attended to as primary ground, language, love, and self. And it does this in the process of creating contradictory impressions even more radical than those in *Pieces*. What we witness is a man growing older, his children growing up and away from him, his wife less surely the one and only person he might love, trying to come or stay together and to come apart.

Unpaginated and divided into two sections, *A Day Book* begins with a dense poetic prose section from which the book takes it title; it then goes on to a section of poetry where formal lyric and smallest fragment create their occasions for speech. Day book, word book, dream book, fuck book, *A Day Book* wishes to make out of its bits and pieces an ark. In *Words*, Creeley had quoted as epigraph a section from William Carlos Williams's poem, "To Daphne and Virginia":

There is, in short

a counter stress,

born of the sexual shock,
which survives it

consonant with the moon,

to keep its own mind.[25]

Like Williams, Creeley draws our attention not only to the link between art and sex but to the riddling fact of the poem or book of poems as "counter stress" or countershock or what Frost would have called "a momentary stay against confusion." Creeley's choice of epigraph for *A Day Book* intimates an intentional strategy of the same kind:

To build itself a hideaway high up in the city,
a room in a tower, timbered with art,
was all it aimed at, if only it might. . . .

"If only it might" raises doubts as much as it points to the will necessary to sustain the enterprise. That Creeley does not include the entire riddle and that he does not reveal the solution (Moon and Sun) suggested by the translator he is using constitute a curious sin of omission.[26] Its discovery only confirms what we know the book was meant to be anyway: Creeley's day and night book, life study, death notebook, cosmogony. But that cosmogony needs the poetic, mystical pact of reader and poet, the assent necessary to make "if only it might" come true. Creeley might also have intended us to find the suppressed solution of the riddle calling to mind two gnomic lines of Blake: "If the Sun and Moon should doubt, / They'd immediately go out."[27] In this light, we discover Creeley's "A Day Book"

25. William Carlos Williams, "To Daphne and Virginia," *Pictures from Brueghel and Other Poems* (New York: New Directions, 1962), p. 78.

26. Michael Alexander, trans., *The Earliest English Poems* (Berkeley: University of California Press, 1970), pp. 134, 207.

27. William Blake, "Auguries of Innocence," *The Poetical Works of William Blake,* ed. John Sampson (London: Oxford University Press, 1958), p. 174.

again confronting the unthinking, assertive fact of the real
as well as the attempt of poetry to make things stay real.
And for a poet like Creeley, the problem of the real inevitably turns him to the problems of creating a loving language
for the finding of an adequate self.

A Day Book, however unorthodox, contains enough for-
mal lyrics, all with defining Creeley strategies — "So Big,"
"A Testament," "The Act of Love," "Time," "People," —
to remind us of some of the best poems of earlier volumes:
"All That is Lovely in Men," "A Wicker Basket," "Kore,"
"The Rain," "The Pool," and "For Love" from For Love,
"I Keep to Myself Such Measures," "The Dream," "Anger,"
"The Window," "To Bobbie," and "Enough" from Words,
"The Finger," "The Moon," "Numbers," and "Could write
of fucking—" from Pieces. But to talk of Creeley's continued
writing and perfecting of his own formal lyric may be to
mistake the intention of Pieces and A Day Book in the same
way that to talk about Creeley and tradition can no longer
be done on the older grounds. Once, Creeley could have
been approached as a poet centrally concerned with a lyric
tradition; in his critical writing, he frequently addressed
those poems or lines of poems—H. D.'s "I go where I love
and am loved ...," Pound's "What thou lovest well remains, / the rest is dross ..." ("Canto LXXXI"), Duncan's
"Often I Am Permitted to Return to a Meadow" — which
he saw as touchstones of a lyric art for locating a locus
and language for love and self. More recently, however,
Creeley has gone out of his way to emphasize a tradition
which I would call, to borrow a phrase from William Carlos
Williams in his Introduction to his own book The Wedge,
"extracurricular."[28] Just as Pieces acknowledged Konrad
Lorenz and R. D. Laing and John Cage and Marshall McLu-
han, so A Day Book gives to the two Alan-Allen figures,
Alan Watts and Allen Ginsberg, a prominence which again
asserts and confirms where Creeley has been moving. Just

---

28. William Carlos Williams, Author's Introduction, The Wedge
(Cummington, Mass.: The Cummington Press, 1944), p. 9.

as Ginsberg has become less concerned with the lyric as
literary mode, Creeley has gone on to write about love in
ways that refuse to distinguish between literature and jot-
ting, poetry and prose, lyric and pornography.

A Day Book is an erotic book, lacking only the photographs of genital and oral love-making which accompany
Creeley's pamphlet poem called His Idea (1973). Here is a
section from the latter poem (on whose opposite page the
couple is making love):

> Note read re
> letter of Lawrence's
>
> to Mrs. Aldous
> Huxley? That
>
> films are obscene
> if when the young
>
> man and woman come home,
> they masturbate one by one.
>
> Not so—
> if they make love.[29]

This passage is crucial to our reading of His Idea and to
A Day Book. But it is the photographless A Day Book to
which I want to circle back. This book has more day-by-
day, night-by-night possibilities than His Idea, whose photographs are limited to one man and one woman anyway.

And how do we react after reading A Day Book? I find
this question as problematic as whether the book is a love
book or a masturbatory fantasy, whether the man in and
behind the book is more open or solipsistic than before,
whether sex for him is more in the "head" or in the "bed."
In order to approach some of these questions, let me expand

---

29. Robert Creeley, His Idea (Toronto: The Coach House Press, 1973),
n. p.

upon the contradictory impressions I earlier suggested *A Day Book* contained.

As in previous books by Creeley, *A Day Book* exposes a man who yearns for the ease of love and the ability to extend that love to a woman: "Now say to her, / love is all" ("So Big"). Love may be all; Creeley wants love to be one of the natural graces, and he spends a lot of time in his sequence, "A Day Book," on things, moments, and people that are beautiful, or, as he calls them, "lovely." Creeley knows that such language risks sentimentality, but he also knows that sentimentality is part of the context of love. At best, Creeley explores sentimentality in relation to the need to acknowledge less sentimental but intensely felt things. Two of the most moving moments in *A Day Book* — Creeley's discovery in a dentist's office that his daughter Sarah, eleven, is a woman; and his retelling of a tale of Allen Ginsberg's about how he couldn't remember someone whose life didn't touch his — reveal important discriminations about affection and love for people whom we do or do not know. Just as it is easy to fail to recognize someone whom we know so well that that person's growth or change might go unnoticed, it is easy to pretend as part of some mistaken love-ethic to love someone whom we do not know at all.

Creeley's discriminations about love and loving, unlike his measure of continuing beat propaganda, provide real strengths in *A Day Book*. In Creeley's fears of love and of his ability to love, however, he creates another and very different impression. This is not only contradictory to much else in the book but it connects with what I have found most nagging and unresolvable in Creeley's work. What we do after reading or seeing *A Day Book* is not so outrageous or inappropriate a question as it might first have seemed.

Here is a section from one of the recent poems in *A Day Book*, a poetic passage which Creeley intends to let stand as a separate, entire poem:

I WANT to fuck you
from two to four

endlessly
the possibility

I want to
fuck you

Charmed
by his own reward.

A trembling now
throughout.

I am here.

The poem's language, imagery, rhythms, and themes reveal
familiar Creeley ground. He wants to move to "here," to
come and say "I am here" as he playfully explores the
meaning of the expression *to come* elsewhere in the book.
The "trembling," a motion which Creeley was attracted to
in earlier poems in earlier volumes, at first seems more
hopeful in this poem. But I am still bothered by the insistence of the "want." In some very basic way, it connects
with a desperate attempt in the book to bring love and love
poem and self, as it is made possible through that act and
fact, into being. Is "I am here" the ecstatic celebration one
interpretation of it would allow? Or is the recurrent "want"
and the ambiguous "trembling" and "Charmed / by his own
reward" suggestive of an incipient insatiability, solipsism,
and convulsiveness which seek to turn the conclusion into
a moment of exhaustion and not the exhaustion which
comes after fulfillment?

There is the danger of slightness in this poem. But the
emotions behind the sparse form are not slight at all. And
the lack of extended attention which *A Day Book* has re-
ceived from the critics might very well be related to this
radical ambiguity, an ambiguity which is as much a matter
of where the poetry and prose are as where Creeley is as
a man. Creeley has always helped to show us how he might
be read, but in *A Day Book* he seems more vulnerable and
unhelpful to the extent that more time goes into describing

the unedited pain of living and loving, more space to unedi-
torially setting forth the impasses attendant upon him as
a middle-aged poet and man. Earlier work of Creeley's had
always bordered on the exposure of uncharming poetry,
at times even of an unpleasant man. The measure of engage-
ment which *A Day Book* manages to elicit from us involves
the same paradox: we often are most engaged by what is
most unengaging of all.

The ending of the sequence, "A Day Book" might just
as well have been part of some other Creeley work or book:

> So of course there was an end to it, even as it began.
> That's what's always known — you feel it even as you
> feel anything, beginning, you have that uncanny, under
> sense, it will end, I can feel it, the wind, already, drops
> a little, a waver, something clear enough. But that hardly
> makes one not want to go, so I always have and will,
> etc. It's nothing new, wanting to be included.

Familiarly, Creeley makes his way *in* his writing and *as*
his writing, "saying / something / as it goes" ("As real as
thinking," *P, 3*). Creeley's "uncanny" or weird sense of the
world; his "under sense" or undersong; his possibilities and
contradictions and qualifications — we have met these all
before. And his "wanting to be included" returns to that
sense I make out to be one of the most important centers
in his work, the wish to be included, wanted, loved; and,
in turn, to include, want, love.

In the context of the sequence, however, and in the context of the entire book, the passage is a darker one. "Clear
enough" is not enough. "Drops a little" is part of that scary
corner of "under sense" in Creeley's world which causes
the rug to bunch under the feet and the sand to gather between the toes. The "etc." is as much a nightmare of proliferation as it is the salvation of possibility.

As a day book, this new collection ought to have lent
itself strategically to the daily and nightly possibility and
variability of love. In the prose and poetry he spends a good
deal of time talking about love, and it is a recurrent word

and theme. And, as I indicated earlier, there are the continuing formal lyrics which we expect Creeley to write. But
the resonance achieved or the residue which remains after
our pushing from Tuesday, November 19, 1968, through to
Friday, June 11, 1971 (his daughter Sarah's graduation day),
speaks of something other than love. What the different
days, dates, weeks, months, years, and places record is the
excruciatingly painful inability of Creeley to leave behind
his cool New England self for his freer Bolinas self, to be
convincingly insistent and persistent in the face of all that
would resist love. Neither drugs nor drink nor Zen nor flirta-
tions with bisexual or androgynous possibility conclude by
adequately clearing "the gunk" (it rhymes with "the junk")
out of his mind, words, and life. At worst, "locate *I* / *love
you*" becomes replaced in *A Day Book* by the wish to return
to some simpler, but finally impossible state. Like the other
three poets in this book, Creeley acknowledges the regres-
sive in both its kinder and more deadly guises. The search
for love and for self gives way to nostalgia for an earlier
life and time recalled early in *A Day Book* by Sascha, a
seventeen-year-old youth in a pastoral world; or, later in
the book's last poem, by his daughter Sarah upon her graduation:

> We live in a circle,
> older or younger,
> we go round
> and around this earth.
>
> I was trying to remember
> what it
> was like
> at your age.

Such nostalgia, although joined to a language of cyclic recurrence and hence comforting assurance for the poet is
still nostalgia. Too tired or bored to say love or fuck again
— "The descriptions are such that he cannot trust them or
rather, would say, fucking is fucking. Having said that, what

to say" — Creeley in *A Day Book* commonly leaves, wrongly as I see it, the present for the past.

However I seek to approach it, *A Day Book* is a sad book. It speaks more of absence than of people who might create a context for love. When Creeley attempts to talk about the human, he sounds too abstract and forgets that the human must always return to particular people, Sascha, Aunt Bernice, Allen, Alan, John (Altoon), Bobbie, who love. Creeley would like us to be convinced that things have eased for him and that he has moved on to a more confident sense of self:

> I've been trying to know what it is to be specifically myself in this point of age, almost asking people how they are feeling in it, as one would fellow travelers in some situation, shipwreck or great happiness, possibly. Such confoundings of myself, in the past, are seemingly now absent. Fears, ways of stating oneself, and so on, do seem truly to have taken themselves off.

But, despite this assertion, the book keeps relentlessly rehearsing the presentation of some small domestic epic in which Creeley still is so singly intent on his own interior, landlocked voyagings that it does not matter whether a faithful Penelope, homecoming, and new self also are part of the plan.

Chapter Four

Sylvia Plath: "Love, Love, My Season"

To locate just what it was that hurt
—Ted Hughes

My mother said, you died like any man.
How shall I age into that state of mind?
—Sylvia Plath, "Electra on the Azalea Path"

Just as the poets discovered the unconscious long before Sigmund Freud, so the extremist poets discovered and were highly conscious of their extremity long before A. Alvarez. One of the remarkable things about poets like Robert Lowell, John Berryman, Robert Creeley, and Sylvia Plath is their relentlessly literate sense of what they are doing and where they are going, however often their achievements and intentions may go amiss or prove to be other than they had thought or hoped they would be. And no poet more than Sylvia Plath keeps reminding us of the terms and the ground of her writing. To say that she writes *in extremis* is not only an accurate statement of fact but a suggestion that more than aesthetic matters may be involved. "The same blue grievances" record a ground-note that the ongoing life of the poet must learn to acknowledge and then manage or not be able to manage at all.

Ariel, Sylvia Plath's major posthumously published book of poems, begins and ends *in extremis.* "Morning Song," the opening poem, begins with the word "love." "Words," the concluding poem, ends on the word "life." The title of the last poem "Words," and the pun in the title of the opening poem "Morning Song" suggest the two other prominent centers here, art and death. Love and death, life and art — these are the extremities out of which the *Ariel* poems proceed. And Plath insisted upon them and returned to them for alignments of the most dangerous kind.

The *Ariel* poems reveal and often pursue a direction more nearly final than that found in Plath's earlier poetry or in her nonpoetic work. What surfaces in *Ariel* proves to be a love of extremity. It expresses itself in obsessive rhythm, in a momentum and an inventiveness of image, and in a defining vocabulary recognizable by what it is attracted to and by what it seeks: totality, finality, obduracy. In Plath's most central books of poetry, *The Colossus* and *Ariel,* the adjectives expose this range of thought and feeling. The attraction involves what is "sheer," "mere," "pure," "absolute," "necessary." Movement in the poems is toward what cannot be stopped or reversed, things "intractable" and "tireless." It is toward what lies beyond loving, human feeling, things "vast" and "immense." And toward what is unrepeatable, things "unique" and "perfect." Plath's recurrent use of the prefixes "in-," "un-," and "ir-" relates to this defining poetics. And her attempt at using words like "terrible," "awful," and "horrible" in their root sense further characterizes her poetry and its preferences. The vocabulary which she evolved in her poetry is never far from the limits her opening and concluding poems announced and made final as the proper centers among which her poems move. How to render and reflect the exactions of such a felt world? Only a radical language would suffice to engage and to encounter such extremity so steadily and unendingly.

The terms under which Plath chose to write her poems are unmistakably given, over and over. She sought to embrace nothing less than "everything." A procedure on this scale was bound to assume personal and historical, aesthetic and sexual dimensions. With implicit, punning awareness of what she might "know," she pretended in her poem, "Zoo Keeper's Wife," that she was "the Tree of Knowledge."[1] Fittingly, in so many of her poems she is busy collecting, confessing, swallowing, and taking in everything:

> I bend over this drained basin where the small fish
> Flex as the mud freezes.
> They glitter like eyes, and I collect them all.
> Morgue of old logs and old images, the lake
> Opens and shuts, accepting them among its reflections.
>   ("Private Ground," CTW, 21)

> The police love you, you confess everything.[2]

> I must swallow it all.
>   ("Maenad," CTW, 51)

> Whatever I see I swallow immediately
> Just as it is, unmisted by love or dislike.
>   ("Mirror," CTW, 34)

> Stupid pupil, it has to take everything in.[3]

If ideally nothing escaped Plath, her tone when confronting what she called "atrocity" or "enormity" shifted between the mocking and the serious, the playful and the deadly. She could play child, adolescent, and adult, alternately, and at the same time. As a consequence, it sometimes is difficult to separate boast from threat or fear from wish in her

---

1. Sylvia Plath, "Zoo Keeper's Wife," *Crossing the Water* (New York: Harper & Row, 1971), p. 39. Hereafter, references to poems in this volume (CTW) will be included in the text.

2. Sylvia Plath, "The Other," *Winter Trees* (New York: Harper & Row, 1972), p. 21. Hereafter, references to poems in this volume (WT) will be included in the text.

3. Sylvia Plath, "Tulips," *Ariel* (New York: Harper & Row, 1966), p. 10. Hereafter, references to poems in this volume (A) will be included in the text.

readiness for the enormity of everything. In some of her poems, she admitted, in a deceptively matter-of-fact kind of statement, the very limits she sought to move beyond:

Some things of this world are indigestible.
("Zoo Keeper's Wife," CTW, 38)

I am incapable of more knowledge.
("Elm," A, 16)

Predictably, the question of knowledge returned the poet to the smaller, but still large questions of love and death, life and art.

What can love manage. What is death's domain. What are the just concerns of life and of art. These involved Plath in the issue not only of poetic content but of poetic form as well.

At once inclusive and exclusive, the content of Sylvia Plath's poetry appropriated all provinces of knowledge. She not only accepted the extremity and enormity of history and personality but sought out the most outrageous facts and *facta* of life and art. Repeatedly, the impression she conveyed was that of a woman and poet to whom nothing was alien. In moving prose written after her death, Ted Hughes, her husband and an important poet himself, attempted to detail this sense in her:

The world of her poetry is one of emblematic visionary events, mathematical symmetries, clairvoyance, metamorphoses, and something resembling total biological and racial recall.[4]

Hughes's last clause defines what readers coming to Plath's work even for the first time inevitably feel. To

---

4. Ted Hughes, "The Chronological Order of Sylvia Plath's Poems," *Tri-Quarterly*, No. 7 (1966), 81. The last clause of the quotation unfortunately was omitted when the piece was redone for *The Art of Sylvia Plath: A Sympoisum*, ed. Charles Newman (Bloomington: Indiana University Press, 1970).

capture this sense, a moment in her own prose would also do. Here, from her short story about a tatoo artist, "The Fifteen-Dollar Eagle," is a daydream description of a dully plain, lily-white character named Laura:

> I have been imagining a lithe, supple Laura, a butterfly poised for flight on each breast, roses blooming on her buttocks, a gold-guarding dragon on her back and Sinbad the Sailor in six colors on her belly, a woman with Experience written all over her, a woman to learn from in this life.[5]

The humor never succeeds in disguising the attraction Plath feels in this story for a figure and a content that is absolute.

What Sylvia Plath sought to manage as content, she also had to handle in and as form. The poetry she admitted admiring and the methods of composition attributed to her by people who knew her involved poems written "all-of-a-piece."[6] Such poems are in evidence in the post-Romantic, organic verse she frequently succeeded in writing, from poems in *The Colossus* to late poems in *Ariel,* and to those now more recently collected in *Crossing the Water* and *Winter Trees.*

If the word "organic" commonly has been turned into an almost meaningless term expressive of a quasi-mystical ideality which is present in a particular poem, for Plath's poetry it can be a critical term of the most descriptive and telling kind. The best poems in her first book, *The Colossus,* are organic in conception, in their management of matters as basic as stanza and line length and image. In the poem, "Man in Black," taken from the first book, Plath achieved a poem unmistakably "all-of-a-piece":

5. Sylvia Plath, "The Fifteen-Dollar Eagle," *The Sewanee Review,* 68 (1960), 617.

6. Sylvia Plath, "Context," *The London Magazine,* 1, No. 11 (1962), 46.

Where the three magenta
Breakwaters take the shove
And suck of the grey sea

To the left, and the wave
Unfists against the dun
Barb-wired headland of

The Deer Island prison
With its trim piggeries,
Hen huts and cattle green

To the right, and March ice
Glazes the rock pools yet,
Snuff-colored sand cliffs rise

Over a great stone spit
Bared by each falling tide,
And you, across those white

Stones, strode out in your dead
Black coat, black shoes, and your
Black hair till there you stood,

Fixed vortex on the far
Tip, riveting stones, air,
All of it, together.[7]

In the last stanza of this poem, the poet draws attention
to a manner of proceeding that lends a persuasive, assertive
finality to so many of the poems she wrote. "Man in Black,"
significantly placed in the midst of poems about the process
or act of poetry — "Strumpet Song," "Snakecharmer," "The
Hermit at Outermost House," "The Disquieting Muses,"
"Medallion" — establishes a unity that is almost mathemat-

---

7. Sylvia Plath, "Man in Black," *The Colossus and Other Poems* (New
York: Alfred A. Knopf, Inc., 1962), pp. 52-53. Hereafter, references to
this American edition (*TC*) will be included in the text.

ical, and hence anticipatory of later poems like "The Night Dances" and "Ariel" from *Ariel*.

By means of a suspended syntax and a sure logic ("to the left," "to the right," "yet," "and you"), the main figure of "Man in Black" rises out of the landscape that anticipates him and that he is part of. Sinister, alien, and deathlike, he joins, like the poet, stasis and rest ("fixed vortex") and earth and heaven ("stones, air"). He stands for the final, lyric image ("on the far/Tip") the Romantic poet strove to confront and to which critics like Frank Kermode have addressed themselves in writing about Romantic or post-Romantic literature.[8] And he serves as that image in the poem. Further, like the Romantic Image, he (it) is both concrete and mysteriously vague ("man in black"), both in a localized ("Deer Island") and nonlocalized (the later stanzas) setting.

What Plath accomplishes in "Man in Black" is nothing less than the achievement, wished for, willed, and executed, of the kind of organic, post-Romantic poem which she delighted in and which she aspired to write. It is, again, in her own words, that poem "born all-of-a-piece," written by poets "possessed by their poems as by the rhythms of their own breathing."[9]

The last line in "Man in Black" — "All of it, together" — succeeds impressively in underlining the impression that the poem has been or at least given the illusion of being "born all-of-a-piece." "Man in Black" concludes by becoming something like a completed miniature "Kubla Khan." The poem is there on the page, "all of it, together." In part, "Man in Black" is one more attempt at writing the final, Romantic poem in the English language.

Another poem in *The Colossus*, "Medallion," creates an impression very much like that of "Man in Black." What is particularly useful about "Medallion" is the ways in which it allows a reader to deduce the development of a

---

8. Frank Kermode, *Romantic Image* (London: Routledge and Kegan Paul, 1957), *passim*.
9. Plath, "Context," 46.

particular kind of poem in the history of British and American poetry. I give the poem in full:

By the gate with star and moon
Worked into the peeled orange wood
The bronze snake lay in the sun

Inert as a shoelace; dead
But pliable still, his jaw
Unhinged and his grin crooked,

Tongue a rose-colored arrow.
Over my hand I hung him.
His little vermilion eye

Ignited with a glassed flame
As I turned him in the light;
When I split a rock one time

The garnet bits burned like that.
Dust dulled his back to ocher
The way sun ruins a trout.

Yet his belly kept its fire
Going under the chainmail,
The old jewels smoldering there

In each opaque belly-scale:
Sunset looked at through milk glass.
And I saw white maggots coil

Thin as pins in the dark bruise
Where his innards bulged as if
He were digesting a mouse.

Knifelike, he was chaste enough,
Pure death's-metal. The yard-man's
Flung brick perfected his laugh.

(TC, 61-62)

"Medallion" is a snake poem, almost a type of subtype in nineteenth- and twentieth-century verse. Behind "Medallion" there are familiar poems like Emily Dickinson's "A Narrow fellow in the Grass" and D. H. Lawrence's "Snake." Since Emily Dickinson and Lawrence are, as eccentric poets or as poets who are part of an eccentric tradition, likely only to offer general affinities with Plath's work, it may be useful to examine these three snake poems in some detail. Similarities as well as important differences in the poets and poems involved will emerge.

The three poems all deal in very special encounters. They deal in a range of experience of psychic or mystical dimensions. All three poets rely upon traditional associations of the snake with matters of knowledge, problems of good and evil, innocence and experience, as much as they attempt to give to their snakes an emblematic, symbolic importance. Emily Dickinson's snake, by the end of the poem, is more than "A narrow fellow in the grass." It becomes a reminder for her of all that sheer being can contain. In much the same way, Lawrence's snake becomes his particular "albatross"; and Plath's snake, her distinguishing "medallion."

The snake of each poet manages to combine attributes at once primitive and civilized, natural and poetic, sexual and aesthetic. Lawrence's snake slowly and surely grows in its associational power. And the "pettiness" of the "I" in the poem — Lawrence's persona and foil to the snake — is considerable enough to demand expiation. Similarly, Dickinson's "transport/Of cordiality" (the root meanings of the Latinates are unmistakable, and at the deeper, nonsyntactical level refer not to Nature's other people, but to the snake) and "Zero at the Bone" — the most intense feelings occasioned by the snake — prove to be demanding and overwhelming, if inevitable. Yet, Dickinson's and Lawrence's poems allow in their framework for the possibility of attitudinized moralizing or distanced philosophizing, which Plath's "Medallion" forgoes. Dickinson and Lawrence see to it that we are sure how we are to respond to the presented experience. Dickinson concludes her poem:

Several of Nature's People
I know, and they know me —
I feel for them a transport
Of cordiality —

But never met this Fellow
Attended, or alone
Without a tighter breathing
And Zero at the Bone —[10]

And here Lawrence concludes his poem, "Snake." This
follows upon his protagonist's having just thrown a log at
the snake (Plath's "flung brick" may be recalling this moment):

And immediately I regretted it.
I thought how paltry, how vulgar, what a mean act!
I despised myself and the voices of my accursed human
    education.

And I thought of the albatross,
And I wished he would come back, my snake.

For he seemed to me again like a king,
Like a king in exile, uncrowned in the underworld,
Now due to be crowned again.

And so, I missed my chance with one of the lords
Of life.
And I have something to expiate;
A pettiness.[11]

"Medallion," in contrast, concludes by being more urgently
immediate in its relentless associations (the snake's "pure

10. Emily Dickinson, The Complete Poems of Emily Dickinson, ed.
Thomas H. Johnson (Boston: Little, Brown and Company, 1960), p. 460.
    11. D. H. Lawrence, The Complete Poems of D. H. Lawrence, ed. Vivian
de Sola Pinto and Warren Roberts (New York: The Viking Press, 1964),
I, 351.

death's-metal" brings together, in a single phrase, perfection and stasis and death), more radically organic in its achievement than the other two poems. Because of its minimal framework, "Medallion" gives us much less help in confronting the complex ambiguity and ambivalence which the entire poem depends upon.

A process is evident in "Medallion" very much like what the critic Robert Langbaum has observed in the poetry of premodern poets like William Blake and Gerard Manley Hopkins, where the reader is less and less able to "see the poet in the process of transferring value to the object."[12] Whatever the similarities of the three snake poems, and they are many, the poems of Dickinson and Lawrence stop short of the movement within "Medallion." That poem takes to a greater limit a range of experience implicit and in part explicit in the other poems.

The bruise, the maggots, and the unhinging laugh never are completely assimilated in "Medallion," and they are never meant to be. The pairs of opposites in the poem (civilized and primitive, natural and crafted, sun and moon) also mark the other poems. But their close and sure accretion here is more controlled and frightening. The ironies of the poem's final "perfected" remain, and they connect with Plath's interest elsewhere in her work in the nature and dangers of perfection.

I am not arguing that "Medallion" is a better poem than the other two. But something has taken place in "Medallion" to the complex matter of tone, to the handling of image, and to the lyrical compression, which makes that poem a very different piece. It is a poem which establishes itself in the development of the purer lyric, away from the narrative, occasional poem tradition in which the other two poems could be comfortably located. In "Medallion," from beginning to end, image has become so internalized and exacting that it is more autonomous than anything we encounter in either of the other poems. "Medallion" comes

---

12. Robert Langbaum, The Poetry of Experience (London: Chatto & Windus, 1957), p. 66.

closer to some sense of what the paramodern poem or what the later poems in *Ariel* or *Crossing the Water* or *Winter Trees* are like.

In the body of Plath's work, "Medallion" connects with that search for adequate image which has become so persistent in modern art. The title, "Medallion," stands for the token or sign connected with the artist and with his art. It is as much a matter of prerogative as of cost. This "medallion" is variously redone in Plath's verse: in the form of a wound that sets the poet apart and turns her into a kind of female Philoctetes; in the form of a scar that she wears as the mark of choice and election, at times in the fashion of a latter-day Emily Dickinson; in the form of an indelible stain or blinding splinter. Also, in the fact of a sweet beesting which she experiences; and in the figure of the albatross (descending from Coleridge to Lawrence to Plath) which becomes the subject and object of her poem "Tulips." Repeatedly, she worries over what the poet can bear and what a poetry can image forth. As a post-Romantic, she knows how her particular medallion or albatross ambiguously offers life and death. In the *Ariel* poems, she wears white (I think of Emily Dickinson again), as a mark of grace as often as a penitential act which she is never sure succeeds.

"Medallion" makes explicit all the risks that involve the poet in the image-making process. It relates to a major concern in *The Colossus*, that is, to build, image by image, a personal and literary structure that will share in creation and health. The last two lines of the last poem, "The Stones," are central:

My mendings itch. There is nothing to do.
I shall be as good as new.

(TC, 84)

Here, the poet looks wishfully and willfully toward some healing process. But this first book never disposes of the question whether this creation will hold or be a ruin, whether its images will be redeeming "stations" or lifeless words. The title poem formulates the enormity of the task for the poet. At the same time, it voices the fear that the woman and the work may never get "put together entirely." Perhaps in the rhyming of "do" with "new" in the lines just quoted from the last poem in The Colossus, there is some of this same uneasy sense. Later poems of hers, collected in the posthumous volumes, increasingly depend upon such heavy, unsettling rhyming.

The early poems, when seen in connection with the poems from the posthumous volumes, reveal a search on the part of the poet for objects or images adequate to whatever love or hate she wished to attach to them. In many of the late poems, she directed her relentless precision toward casting poems in the form of extended correlatives. In the first line of each poem, an interior state commonly is recorded toward which the rest of the movement of the poem is painstakingly devoted. Note the shared direction in the first lines of "Tulips," "The Swarm," and "A Birthday Present":

The tulips are too excitable, it is winter here.

$$(A, 10)$$

Somebody is shooting at something in our town.

$$(A, 64)$$

What is this, behind this veil, is it ugly, is it beautiful?

$$(A, 42)$$

Each poem exposes a search for adequate image.[13] Each exposes the wish to find whatever is in the vase or in the tree or behind the veil. In the course of each poem the poet steadily attempts "to locate just what it was that hurt."[14] These were Ted Hughes's words to describe that activity

---

13. I dealt briefly with matters of adequacy and the poetry of Sylvia Plath in my article, "The Modern British and American Lyric: What Will Suffice," Papers on Language & Literature, 8 (1972), 85-88.

14. Hughes, "Notes on the Chronological Order of Sylvia Plath's Poems," p. 191.

or process which is more and more observable in the *Ariel* poems, but in which, beginning with some of the later poems of *The Colossus,* Hughes saw her as already consciously engaged.

The poems "Tulips" and "The Swarm" and "A Birthday Present" are not just attempts at clarification and concretion. Something even more extreme than noncommunication or failed relationships, matters common to so much narrowly confessional poetry, is in evidence. These poems record situations *in extremis,* situations in which the poet's hold on things and on people and events has become increasingly unsure. The world looks fluorescent, foggy, and cheerlessly nursery-talelike. Specifically, what surfaces is a crisis of correspondence at so primary a level of word and thing that the poem turns, in part, into a wild tour-de-force of image-making to bring life or death.

In "Tulips," Sylvia Plath pursues an unflinching logic which uncovers whatever significance possibly can be exhumed from this woman (the "I" of the poem) and these flowers. The poem begins as a hospital poem, a piece which has become almost a subtype in confessional verse. But, from the first line, there is also the sense that so simple a description of "Tulips" will never suffice. The persona is marked by a wound that is not just a wound but an infinite hurt. In the course of the poem, the poet tries to work out, in a seemingly unending progression of metaphor, what these flowers have to do with the woman (the "I") and with her hurt. The tulips assume an existence and an energy of their own. Finally, they consume whatever chances for health and life they held out to her and of which they reminded her. The tulips bestow on her both privilege and deprivation. They are "albatross" and "communion tablet," at the same time that they consume her breath and body. By the conclusion of the poem, Plath manages to associate the flowers with objects that range, radically, from huge, African cats to rust-red engines. Ingenious and desperate, "Tulips" paradoxically establishes its winnowing precision in the very act of calling up a long line of correspondences.

Although not a hospital poem, "The Swarm" proceeds

from a common center. Like "Tulips," it gives the impression of coming "from a country far away as health." "The Swarm," to alter the metaphor slightly, is a nest of poems. It is suggestive of "Tulips" in the kind of mad, associational and metaphysical triumph toward which it also moves. In "The Swarm," Napoleon and Europe and bee-shooting merge. And historical comment alternately proves satiric, philosophical, and lyric. But the historical conceits of the poem are a deflection of the extremely personal nature of the poem. The careful, gradual building of the lines comes to focus in the last stanzas upon the "I" of the poem. Things as disparate as exile in Elba and the swarm-keeper finally come together and bear down upon the speaker of the poem:

> Pom! Pom! "They would have killed me."
>
> (A, 65)

"The Swarm," when included in the American edition of *Ariel,* significantly was located among her bee poems. In its strategies, "The Swarm" stands in the body of Plath's work as one more attempt to locate what hurts, to find correlatives adequate to the "something" and "somebody" of the first line of the poem. The frightening ambiguity of the "they" ("They would have killed me") exposes not only an important direction in the other bee poems, but in much of her other work. "The Swarm" ends by providing its own narrowing reduction to *"me,"* its own variant of argument between self and other.

As Plath pursues image in "Tulips" and "The Swarm," there is as much sense of movement toward vision as there is the fearful threat of ecstasy which, then, sadly fails to appear. "A Birthday Present" also deals with the problematic appearance of vision. To locate what lies behind the veil determines the progression of the entire poem. But the tense is always optative — what the experience, life-giving and death-giving, life-taking and death-taking, might be like. At once, vision is seen as sexual, aesthetic, and mystical.

In "A Birthday Present," Sylvia Plath focuses upon the metaphor of the gift and upon its possible arrival or failure to emerge. As in the case of the other two poems, the title of "A Birthday Present" indicates what is the central metaphor. It, too, uncompromisingly drives that metaphor through a seemingly endless series of variations. And it does this in the act of questioning, repeatedly, whether any correlative is adequate for what the poet wishes to express. In the development of the poem, the image of the birthday present embraces, by means of the logic of dream or free association, that inclusive-exclusive property of being natural and artificial, familiar and distantly exotic. As part of a surrealistic, sexual-mystical fantasy, the birthday present is ivory tusk and adding machine. It is knife and cry.

The hurtful redness of the tulips, like the potential risk of a bee-sting or of a birthday present, never prevents Plath from seeking some imaged equivalent for that hurt. These governing images embody what she painfully located as much as they offer promises of release from the same pain. If language threatens to become a weapon which could turn against the poet, it also is courted as exorcism in these poems.

Plath associates, implicitly or explicitly, tulips and bees and birthday present with words or with the activity of image-making. The poet finds words to be simultaneously attractive and repelling. They can both kill and save. In the figure of the honey-making activity of the bees in "The Swarm" and of the cycle of the queen bee in her other bee poems, she is able to bring together in a single image the life-death, honey-sting drama of bees and words.

Separately and as a group, the three poems deal with problems of language, or, more specifically, with the adequacy of any image in the face of an extreme situation. They address the confrontation, immediate or potential, of something desired, yet also feared. And they address the problem of finding words able to express that confrontation. In each of these poems, the poet attempts to locate, by means of a run of images, what "it" is: in "Tulips," what "it" is that is in the vase and to what "it corresponds," a correspondence which signals sickness or health, life or death; in "The Swarm," what "it" is that is in the tree and, in the mind, so intriguing and threatening at the same time; in "A Birthday Present," what "it" is that can lie behind the veil and be the source of such comforting and horrible enormity.

"Tulips," "The Swarm," and "A Birthday Present" are not anomalies in seeking out what "it" is. This search serves as an occupation and preoccupation throughout all of Plath's verse. As if her naming of "it" would break some taboo which must continue to be observed, she keeps indicating in these and other poems how "it" can never be penetrated. Like the concentration-camp horrors to whose enormity the poet obsessively returns, "it" can be intimated, addressed, but, in the end, never completely embodied. And, in terms of the poetry, necessarily so. For although the "it" trades in first and last things, she suggests that nothing as aggregate or generalized as life or love or death ever could contain it. It simply is.

The need to locate what "it" is proves equally central to the movement and meanings of other poems of Plath's. In part, the mad and associational intensity of poems like "Lady Lazarus," "Daddy," and "The Applicant" becomes understandable in view of what the poet, there, is bent on relentlessly seeking out:

I have done it again.
One year in every ten
I manage it.

(A, 6)

They always *knew* it was you.
Daddy, daddy, you bastard, I'm through.

(A, 51)

A living doll, everywhere you look.
It can sew, it can cook,
It can talk, talk, talk.

It works, there is nothing wrong with it.
You have a hole, it's a poultice.

You have an eye, it's an image.
My boy, it's your last resort.
Will you marry it, marry it, marry it.

                                                                    (A, 5)

Again, the location and formulation of what "it" is concerns
the poet. The lines quoted above all occur strategically.
They are placed at the beginning or at the end, whether
ultimate or penultimate, of the poems in which they appear.
And each poem's major energies are engaged in building
both toward and away from what "it" happens to be. At
times, there is the sense that the poet has located "it." But,
in the end, this impression turns illusory or uncertain. In
"Lady Lazarus," for example, "it" fails to emerge when the
suicide attempts fail. At the conclusion of the poem, the
chances of defining or transcending "it" suggest childish
threat or dare as much as the confident will toward its execu-
tion:

    Herr God, Herr Lucifer,
    Beware
    Beware.

    Out of the ash
    I rise with my red hair
    And I eat men like air.

                                                                    (A, 9)

In a similar manner, the concluding rhythms of the poems
"The Applicant" and "Daddy" present ambiguities which
are substantial enough to make us question whether Plath
ever had found or ever could have found the image with
which she sought to "marry" or exorcize "it". Sometimes
I wonder whether she ever asked or asked adequately what
it was she was "marrying" or "married" to.
    Basically, all these poems address the nature of image-
making and the adequacy or inadequacy of the poet in the
face of that process. What distinguishes "The Applicant"
from the start is the extent to which image-making stands

as the central metaphor and central theme of the poem.

Throughout, "The Applicant" explicitly establishes a connection between "image" and a nonreducible "it." In the poem, Plath underwrites what so many of her poems are about, the establishment of radical correspondences between life (love) and death, person and image, poet and poem. "The Applicant" might well have stood as the first or last poem in *Ariel,* except that the poems which occupy those places, "Morning Song" and "Words," are also concerned with matters as essential and passionate as life and art. "The Applicant," when looked at as parable and conceit, can be shown to hold the mirror up to the image-making process. And infinitely to complicate the process because of the complexity and variety of the mirror. Invention, including the invention of images, also is basic here. The elaborate cloud-mirror-wind image of "Morning Song," and the pool-face-star image of "Words," find restatement in the particular variations that "The Applicant" plays upon the activity of image-creation. In part, "The Applicant" recalls "The Stones" and "The Colossus," poems from her first volume.

The figure in "The Applicant," who gives the poem its title, seeks an image or eye ("I") which will establish self. Essentially, that marriage or union is what image-making is all about. In the poems, "Daddy" and "Lady Lazarus," Plath repeats the concern evident in "The Applicant" for locating images adequate to some inordinate hurt. In the search for such images, the poet knows everything is at stake.

Always, in the act of image-making, what the poet engages through images are things regal and sacred, although neither political nor religious in actual fact. In an interview, Plath said:

Surely the great use of poetry is its pleasure — not its influence as religious or political propaganda. Certain poems and lines of poetry seem as solid and miraculous to me as church altars or the coronation of queens must seem to people who revere quite different images.[15]

Here, the language of the prose may very well be echoing Yeats in his poem "Among School Children," where the process of image-making provides the unifying theme. In Yeats's poem, the nun, mother, philosopher, and poet inevitably deal with images. Image-making proves to be a defining, inescapable activity for man. And the poet as image-maker comes to stand for the poet as ideal man.

If "The Applicant," "Daddy," and "Lady Lazarus" reveal Plath centrally concerned with the universal habit of image-making, this is not all. More important, in these poems she exhibits the extremes, personal and historical, to which image-making has been taken.

"Daddy" and Lady Lazarus" extend and provide variations on the concerns of "The Applicant." In particular, they seek to locate what it was that hurt. These two poems radically confront Lear-like questions of man and his image, of what constitutes for him need and excess. "Is man no more than this? Consider him well," Lear mused. Both "Lady Lazarus" and "Daddy" raise issues as basic as image and as man. They seek to find images which will sufficiently body forth that man.

"Lady Lazarus" and "Daddy" are poems which seem written at the edge of sensibility and of imagistic technique. They both utilize an imagery of severe disintegration and dislocation. The public horrors of the Nazi concentration camps and the personal horrors of fragmented identities become interchangeable. Men are reduced to parts of bodies and to piles of things. The movement in each poem is at once historical and private; the confusion in these two spheres suggests the extent to which this century has often made it impossible to separate them. Belsen implies private man in the same way that the modern, psychiatric-officed city implies historical Belsen.

---

15. Plath, "Context," p. 46.

The barkerlike tone of "Lady Lazarus" is not accidental. As in "Daddy," the persona strips herself before the reader — or viewer turned voyeur — all the time utilizing a cool or slang idiom in order to disguise feeling. Sylvia Plath borrowed from a sideshow or vaudeville world the respect for virtuosity which the performer must acquire, for which the audience pays and never stops paying. Elsewhere in her work, she admired the virtuosity of the magician's unflinching girl or of the unshaking tattoo artist. Here, in "Lady Lazarus," it is the barker and the striptease artist who consume her attention. What the poet persues in image and in rhyme (for example, the rhyming of "Jew" and "gobbledygoo") becomes part of the same process I observed in so many of her other poems, that attempt, brilliant and desperate, to locate what it was that hurt.

"Lady Lazarus" and "Daddy" move toward locating some final image to define the woman (poet) or man (father, god) who figures so prominently in all of her work. The imagery of "statue" and "model" in "Daddy" draws attention to what both poems seek out, some final image adequate to contain what she must confront. The search for final images establishes a connection between poet and Nazi which comments upon a reductionist, absolute method finally leading to madness. What the Nazis strove to do, to reduce Jew and Aryan to some final image, caused each to become a parody of essential humanity. The risks for the historical idealist-madman and for the extremist poet merge in that relentless pursuit of, image by image, the final man or final poem, stripped of everything but what will not burn in the crucible of mind and oven:

I am your opus,
I am your valuable,
The pure gold baby

That melts to a shriek.
I turn and burn.
Do not think I underestimate your great concern.

Ash, Ash —
You poke and stir,
Flesh, bone, there is nothing there —

A cake of soap,
A wedding ring,
A gold filling.

("Lady Lazarus," A, 8)

One central meaning of the poem is clear. Any image, pursued as far as can go, evolves into a nightmare which concludes by abandoning whatever human circumference it
may have originally ostensibly claimed. That nightmare is
at once aesthetic and historical.

The kind of imagery and imagistic movement evident in
"Daddy" and "Lady Lazarus" bring these poems closer to
"The Applicant" than a reader might have at first imagined.
The poems complement one another as well as serve as
attempts to intimate, if not realize, what that final poem
would be like in which adequate correlatives had been
found. What this achievement would involve, in cost and
loss, the linkage of image-making Nazi and poet shows.

"Childless Woman" and "Thalidomide," poems written
during the time of the *Ariel* poems but included in *Winter
Trees,* take a reader as close to the image-making process
as he is likely ever to come. Both poems are built upon
some of the same deadly associations of other poems at
which I have been looking. They posses an immediacy and
urgency which suggest that they are occurring in some si-
multaneous present where creation is in process:

Spiderlike, I spin mirrors,
Loyal to my image,

Uttering nothing but blood —
Taste it, dark red!

("Childless Woman," WT, 34)

All night I carpenter

A space for the thing I am given,
A love

Of two wet eyes and a screech.
                        ("Thalidomide," WT, 23-24)

But as each poem proceeds to its conclusion, the poet is
unable to bring into being the love or the child or foetus-
poem she has tried to bring to light. Instead, "Childless
Woman" and "Thalidomide" end by finding only images
of death, both a murderous forest of blood and a white,
masturbatory presence:

And my forest

My funeral,
And this hill and this
Gleaming with the mouths of corpses.
                        ("Childless Woman," WT, 34)

White spit

Of indifference!
The dark fruits revolve and fall.

The glass cracks across,
The image

Flees and aborts like dropped mercury.
                        ("Thalidomide," WT, 24)

The final image in "Thalidomide" is one of a sickroom ther-
mometer full of images which crack and flee, drop and
abort. What is disturbing about the two poems is how each
moves toward moments where final images almost emerge
and perhaps even do. It is as if Plath leaves behind some
ideal image, which would still grow out of a human, loving

context, for some image so sheer and absolute that it necessarily brings death. In part, the poet is so successful in these poems in finding final images that they prove to be imageless and life-destroying. In "Childless Woman," the "I" finally is so "loyal" to her image that she gains death. In "Thalidomide," she is able in the course of the poem to achieve the abolition of correspondence and metaphor. The image, sought, has such luminosity that it is imageless. "Negro, masked like a white," that final image possesses the absence of black and white.

"Childless Woman" and "Thalidomide" raise to a metaphoric level what menstruation and an unsafe tranquilizer can signify and bring to a woman, the loss or deformation of the image-foetus. Or, to shift the terms of talking about these poems to a more historically literary level, "Childless Woman" and "Thalidomide" establish what the extremities of a post-Romantic image-making continually held for Plath, the threat of death implicit in the necessarily desperate act of the poet in the pursuit of images. Yet they are images which could also bring correspondence and love. How much the entire body of Plath's poetry sought to carpenter images, "a space for the thing I am given,/A love," we shall see only too soon.

> They will roll me up in bandages, they will store my heart
> Under my feet in a neat parcel
> —Sylvia Plath, "Last Words"

> It was my love that did us both to death
> —Sylvia Plath, "Electra on the Azalia Path"

After Plath's suicide and the posthumous publication of *Ariel,* critics and friends, in writing about her, were insistent in celebrating her generosity and her capacity for happiness and love. In part, it was as if they thought the poems might offer first impressions of another, very different kind. Ted Hughes, in his note to the Poetry Book Society's selection of *Ariel,* attended to the establishment of this same sense of her as woman and poet of love:

What she was most afraid of was that she might come to live outside her genius for love, which she also equated with courage, or "guts," to use her word. This genius for love she certainly had, and not in the abstract. She didn't quite know how to manage it: it possessed her. It fastened her to cups, plants, creatures, vistas, people, in a steady ecstasy. As much of all that as she could, she hoarded into her poems, into those incredibly beautiful lines and hallucinatory evocations.

In these comments, Hughes moves toward finding an image for her as much as he reveals fears, including Plath's own fears, whether she could ever "manage" such love. Tellingly, the word "manage" occurs in some of her poems where questions of love are most painfully at stake.

"Love set you going like a fat gold watch" fittingly stands as the opening line in the opening poem, "Morning Song," *Ariel*. It introduces the willful movement toward love and, as the poem continues, the difficulty of its reality and presence.

Throughout the *Ariel* poems, love and the poet's need and often lack of it are thematically and dramatically prominent. In "I Want, I Want," an earlier poem from *The Colossus*, Plath may be recalling William Blake's engraving by that title (from *The Gates of Paradise*) where a diminutive figure has a ladder pointed to the distant, longed-for stars. And in "Sheep in Fog," one of the *Ariel* poems, Plath wrote her own version of the Twenty-Third Psalm, but without Lord (both father and Father) and with "want." The poems "I Want, I Want" and "Sheep in Fog" are responses to a generalized situation of man as a desiring creature. At worst, there is something vaguely literary about them. At best, they connect with what became for Plath an increasingly urgent and intense need for radical correspondence and sheer love.

By the time the *Ariel* poems were written, Sylvia Plath had moved beyond love as something often distractingly allusive, to love and all of its gradations as they centrally affected her. "A labor of love, and that labor lost," she wrote in "Point Shirley," a poem from *The Colossus*. It was written for her grandmother and related importantly to herself.

Later, the same wit and intelligence were joined to concerns closer to her own life and self and art. She would learn, as she had not yet fully learned in the moving but still allusive "Point Shirley" poem, just how far and for how long she could afford to depart from the real, unmistakable center of her work.

Near the end of her life, love became an inordinately complicated and difficult matter, but Plath never had written simple love poems or regarded love as a feeling or concept she could easily handle. The Colossus poems, the Ariel poems, and the poems now collected in Crossing the Water and Winter Trees, all attest to the wish to turn poetry into loving measures, so many loving, counting procedures. But, variously, love was for her a gift and a curse, a red presence and a white absence. She could never be very sure what love was and whether it was actual or even wanted. From the very first, her poetry showed an attraction to the personas of spinsters, widows, and childless women, all figures cut off from love or its realization. In the early poems, these personas often are literary. Still, the attraction to them is evident and important. What happens in the late poems is that these figures are transformed from potentially Romantic trappings into loveless women more tellingly related to the poet herself.

Sylvia Plath never stopped recording in her poetry the wish and need to clear a space for love. Yet she joined this to an inclination to see love as unreal, to accompanying fears of being unable to give and receive love, and to the eventual distortion and displacement of love in the verse. Loving completely or "wholly" she considered to be dangerous, from her earliest verse on.

Love was so much a part of her world that it often stood in her poetry for that world itself. When the world seemed unreal, so did love. In the early poetry, this sometimes approximated a secondhand, Romantic poetics. But the early poems also give evidence of some more profound sense of a loving unreality which the later poems turned into a more desperate, pathetic tableau of "valentine-faces" and candy or enamel-painted hearts.

Plath often wrote with humor and irony when she considered love. She could be the satirist alert to the sentiments of a Victorian or Edwardian age. She could be a shrewd psychologist of love's ambiguities. She could be sane and clairvoyant, joining writers as major as Shakespeare and Dostoyevsky in probing the darkness of the heart. But in what she wrote just before and at the time of *Ariel,* she began to establish a stance which I find problematic and dangerous. A progression is evident in her handling of love and the love poem that calls into question the loving intentions which some of the first lines of poems announce, but which the tone of whole poems or the endings of poems commonly belie.

"Love" recurs as a word throughout *Ariel.* Yet, in fact, love is most often absent in the poems which seek it most. In several poems, "love" is repeated as address and as apostrophe:

Love, love, my season.
> ("The Couriers," A, 2)

Love, love,
I have hung our cave with roses.
With soft rugs —

The last of Victoriana.
> ("Nick and the Candlestick," A, 34)

Love, love, the low smokes roll
From me like Isadora's scarves, I'm in a fright

One scarf will catch and anchor in the wheel.
> ("Fever 103°," A, 53)

In each case, there is something that turns mad and desperate. There ensues an unconvincing, unsuccessful volitionalism which poets like Lowell, Berryman, and Creeley also evidence in their work. Love is willed and summoned and invoked. But it does not arrive or it is noticeably absent.

Related to the extremity of Plath's attempts to create and claim love is the nature of that need. Her need proves to be beyond the human, suggestively unhuman or inhuman in some poems, as much as it connects with her fears that her heart may be "too small" or that she may not find objects sufficient for her "excessive love." What her husband Ted Hughes wrote of her fears for love, the poems also record. In the important *Ariel* bee poems, her uncertainty issues in the fear of being hurt or fatally "stung" by love. It is the kind of bad joke or bad pun which comes to typify her late art. It expresses a situation so extreme and intolerable to her that only by such devices could she ever have hoped to manage her world. Lowell and Berryman use similar devices, but very often out of real strength. In Plath, however, the strategy commonly reduces to sheer helplessness.

The *Ariel* poems reveal a woman both too exposed and too unopen. The sexuality is relentless and overwhelming. The puns not only proliferate — "head," "queen," "screw," "cherry" — but succeed in words like "mail" (letter and "male") and "box" (sexual organ and coffin) in making explicit the meanings which are central to her work. Like so many older moderns and her contemporaries, Plath underlines on these occasions the links between sexuality and aesthetics, death and love.

As Plath looks at love in the *Ariel* poems, she lends to figures in those poems a desperate need for love which is often joined to its absence or distortion. She gives to one of the pair in "Death & Co." three lines which could serve as epigraph and epitaph for the entire volume:

Bastard
Masturbating a glitter,
He wants to be loved.

(*A*, 28)

Elsewhere, this desperation receives confirmation in her recurrent disbelief that love does or can exist. "My heart/it really goes," she coyly and pathetically has to assure her readers who, by this time, may be feeling like voyeurs.

In one poem, she asks in wondering disbelief how love ever did "get here." And, in another, part as boast and part as amazement to herself, she asks whether her readers are aware of the miracle offered. And the punctuation makes the question into an assertion:

Does not my heat astound you. And my light.

("Fever 103," A, 54)

In still another, she intimately and with great understatement confides:

Do not think I underestimate your great concern.

("Lady Lazarus," A, 8)

And, again, the deadly, playful tone is central.

Frequently, her wish and great need to love are complicated by a counterimpulse toward abstraction and number whose logic ultimately is that of blood. "Magi," a poem included in *Crossing the Water*, finds its major movements and meanings in the dramatic tension between the impulse toward mathematical "abstracts" and toward "Love the mother of milk." It is upon that first, unloving logic or movement that the poems of *Ariel* rely most:

But in twenty-five years she'll be silver,
In fifty, gold.

("The Applicant," A, 5)

This is Number Three.
What a trash
To annihilate each decade.

("Lady Lazarus," A, 6)

Two, of course there are two.
It seems perfectly natural now.

("Death & Co.," A, 28)

She'll cut her throat at ten if she's mad at two.

("Lesbos," A, 30)

Behind these poems is the logic that led to the concentration camps — the piles of silver and gold fillings, the planned destruction of millions, the acceptance of anything as natural and reasonable. It is also the loveless, mistaken logic of Regan to Lear on the subject of attendants — "What need one?"

More serious threats to love become obvious in the *Ariel* poems in what exists as Plath's central, controlling metaphor for the world and, in turn, for men and women in that world. Her choice of metaphor again, as always, defines the possibilities or impossibilities for love.

The *Ariel* poems, even the earlier pieces, take as their central images the world as concentration-camp oven, museum, mausoleum, deadly honey-machine, bell jar, madhouse, sideshow, and dollhouse. These depend upon correspondences and correlations of the most intimate kind. She killed herself by oven gas. The word "museum" is contained within the word "mausoleum." The bell jar, both preserver of delicate, precious, rarefied things and possible suffocating object, also served as the title of the novel which she wrote and published. The deadly honey-machine connects both with her father who was an international expert on bumblebees and with herself as a woman who kept bees in Devon. The world as madhouse gains weight from her personal mental history. And the world as dollhouse and sideshow is made resonant by the biographical image of the Smith student who could do anything, even (and especially) talk, and of the woman who felt herself more and more open and on display. Beyond this rationale for the choice of the particular metaphor, however, lies their collective force and their appropriateness for whatever vision she held of the world. And, beyond that, lies the even larger metaphor of the world as prison and hospital. They are the images implicit in all of the other images, and they exist as images in their own right in many of her poems.

If Plath wished her poems to stand as love letters to the

world, the perspective from which they proceed may, in the end, have made that wish impossible. Her metaphor for the world may very well have been a response to a loveless world. But it is here that the logic of the argument breaks down. For the poetry shows the controlling metaphor threatening to become the informing vision itself. By the time she wrote her last poems, there was less and less room for and patience with love. If the poems were once meant to create love, they came to stand for a world which had forgone or gone beyond some loving, human circumference.

The problem of artistic control which so many critics have addressed in Sylvia Plath I find less central and settleable than that of the controlling metaphor in her verse. Her best poems are incredibly controlled. But the issue of controlling metaphor lingers on long after a reader has decided whether the poems show control or "the look of control" or "controlled uncontrolledness."

The controlling metaphor affects much that happens in Plath's poetry. In the process of finding what to "do" with her love, she often concluded by inverting it. Poem by poem, not just in *Ariel*, she radically confused love and death, self and other. Images of love give way to images of incest ("Daddy," and the bee poems) and masturbation ("Suicide Off Egg Rock," "Ariel," "Death & Co.," "The Jailor," "Childless Woman"). Loveless images of madness, suicide, and solipsism — from the "I am, I am, I am" of "Suicide Off Egg Rock" to the "ich, ich, ich, ich" of "Daddy" — take on the force of leitmotifs for her work. And art, if capable of leading us back to loving, human contexts, here gives the impression of being one more inversion of love. It can be one more deception in this life.

In the late poems, something happens to language and to love and to the possibility of defining a self through love. Repeatedly, the health or breakdown of one is a reflection of the other. In "Suicide Off Egg Rock," a poem from *The Colossus*, the poet associated the approaching destruction of self in suicide and the failure of words:

The words in his book wormed off the pages.
Everything glittered like blank paper.

(36)

What preceded the suicide — the loveless solipsism of "I am, I am, I am" — joins the final, masturbatory image of the sea which now has the protagonist in loving, loveless death:

He heard when he walked into the water

The forgetful surf creaming on those ledges.

(36)

Deadly associations of this kind increase in the poems from *Ariel, Crossing the Water,* and *Winter Trees.* They are prominent in *The Bell Jar* and in those short stories of hers which take the dissolution of love, loving self, and art also as their themes.

As a representative, twentieth-century writer, Plath lends to ,language as language a central place in her work. But in the implications and concluding achievement of this, she is entirely herself. In five very late poems, "Words," "Kindness," "Edge," "Contusion," and "The Fearful," she has no rival, perhaps fortunately so.

These poems, unlike "Lesbos" or "Stillborn" which show love and language breaking down but which discover no words or tone artful enough to manage that fact, succeed in what they attempt. They learn the art of leaving human love behind, but whether out of necessity or freedom it is not always clear.

The five poems share, aside from having been written during the last week of Plath's life, an assessment of a situation where love seems either absent or unreal, deceptive or unimportant. In all of them, there is a rightness in choice of phrase and word and a brilliance in the run of images in individual stanzas and in entire poems. An ease appears, very much like that achieved in the opening of poems like "Death & Co." and "The Manor Garden."

At the same time, however, the assured matter-of-factness of these poems reveals and underlines what words have become — "worms in the glottal stops" in the case of "The Fearful"[16]; and wounds, in the case of "Contusion":

Colour floods to the spot, dull purple.

(A, 83)

The poem, "Words," uncovers an equally desperate state of affairs. As the concluding poem in *Ariel,* it seeks to recover correspondence:

The sap
Wells like tears, like the
Water striving
To re-establish its mirror
Over the rock

That drops and turns,
A white skull,
Eaten by weedy greens.

(85)

But the strategy or magic never works. Love's hooves, which the poet of "Elm" had found gone, also desert her here in the form of "hoof taps" which sound of separation and loss:

Words, dry and riderless,
The indefatigable hoof-taps.
While
From the bottom of the pool, fixed stars
Govern a life.

(85)

The word "while" might have reversed the movement and

---

16. Sylvia Plath, "The Fearful," included with "Edge," "Kindness," "Contusion," and a short note by A. Alvarez in "A Poet's Epitaph," *The Observer,* 17 February 1963, p. 23.

sent the poet back to loving, redeeming language. But it does not. For the final image is that of Narcissus, staring into a pool, mistaking wordless stasis for "fixed stars."

These poems all take an associational, imagistic technique to a point of deadly confusion and delusion where the poet can fold her poem-children back into her body simply by writing out the wish ("Edge") or where she is so uncomprehending of human, loving kindness that she cannot distinguish between children and roses ("Kindness").

What I am suggesting is that these late poems are not the mystically calm, orderly pieces which some critics have seen them to be. Instead, they are the terrible, terrifying creations of a woman who, near the end of a life, still could not do without love, even if she never learned what to do with it. As a result, the tone of the poems is something less than the matter-of-factness of the saint. If Plath saw one of her totems, the moon, "used to this sort of thing," she was never totally easy in moving to a dimension beyond love. And the opening of her very late poem, "Edge," in which she considered the moon in this cool, transcendent light, calls into question the very necessity — stasis, death, perfection — which this and other poems of hers celebrate and dignify:

> The woman is perfected.
> Her dead
>
> Body wears the smile of accomplishment,
> The illusion of a Greek necessity
>
> Flows in the scrolls of her toga,
> Her bare
>
> Feet seem to be saying:
> We have come so far, it is over.

(A, 84)

"The illusion of a Greek necessity." "Seem to be saying." If this is necessity, it is not freedom. There is too much doubt for freedom, and too little saving irony to create a more human art.

In "Kindness," one of her other poems from this group, there are similar complications in perspective. Love's deceptive sweetness was always an obsessive image in her verse. In "Kindness," she attempted to write from a perspective which mocked "sugar" (love) as "a necessary fluid." But, as in other poems, the tone is sad and shrill. Importantly, if she was less and less able to recognize and realize love in her art and her life, it was never completely renounced by her.

If love was never completely renounced by her, neither was it constant in her work. And the poems keep recording a journey and a movement as inevitable as death. Now that the poems which were written just before or at the same time as the *Ariel* poems have been collected and published in *Crossing the Water* and *Winter Trees*, we are afforded an even better means of charting and confirming larger movements and stages in her work.[17] When Ted Hughes and other critics first wrote of an inevitable, conscious development in her poetry and when the titles of the posthumous books *Crossing the Water* and *Winter Trees* were first announced, I wondered how willful was the creation of that legendary development and reputation. But a consideration of the poems themselves and of her title, *The Colossus*, for her first book, helped to dispel such fears. In the same way, interpretations of her art after the fact of her suicide now strike me as less arbitrary and fallacious than they once did. That she eventually took her own life is important. It might be dangerous not to consider that fact seriously.

Plath's development from *The Colossus* to the poems of the later volumes is technical as much as it is psychic and

---

17. Marjorie Perloff has pointed out problems of dating and inaccuracies of editing in a number of the poems included in *Crossing the Water* and *Winter Trees*. But her argument does not affect the particular poems I use to support my own argument about the journey which Sylvia Plath's poetry records. See Marjorie Perloff, "Extremist Poetry: Some Versions of the Sylvia Plath Myth," *Journal of Modern Literature*, 2 (1972), 585-588. Perloff makes the same points in "On the Road to *Ariel*: The 'Transitional' Poetry of Sylvia Plath," *The Iowa Review*, 4, No. 2 (1973), 94-96.

spiritual. More particularly, that development concerns her use of image in connection with the possibilities for language and love. How that development implies and makes explicit a journey, her gathered work actualizes and clarifies.

By the title of her first volume, *The Colossus,* Plath signified what she would spend a lifetime trying to create. Sometimes she exchanged the colossus image for the image of an ark or a garden. But the intentions were always the same, to write words that would bear love and that would have life. The difficulty, however, was that, from the very beginning, her landscape risked turning into (to use images from her own poems) some nightmarish bestiary or wintering ship or burnt-out spa. The problem of what would be her controlling metaphor, then, was full upon her from her earliest work.

The poems she wrote after those included in *The Colossus* show her still involved in trying to put together saving, loving words. But the colossus which she feared would never get "put together entirely" and which she feared would be a ruin becomes more than a distant, playful fear. The opening and closing poems of *The Colossus* — "The Manor Garden" and "The Stones" — depend upon and establish the essential, ominous ambiguity that mark later poems like "Tulips." "Tulips," ending on the word, "health," records the wishful movement in which the poet would like to engage:

> The water I taste is warm and salt, like the sea,
> And comes from a country far away as health.
>
> (A, 12)

But loving "health," like life-giving "salt," is limited by a syntactical and spiritual context which, in the end, disallows and disavows it.

Now that *Crossing the Water* and *Winter Trees* have been published, there is the opportunity to observe the poet at every stage taking stock of her situation and development.

The *Colossus* and *Ariel*, even before the other volumes appeared recently, showed her charting a course, or "getting there," as she put it; she assigned it as a title to one of her poems. If the exact nature of the journey or voyage or ride, all prominent metaphor in her verse, was often in doubt, its connection with love was not.

There are two major movements which the entire body of Plath's poetry suggests — toward the creation of love and toward some state beyond love. These movements are not strictly chronological any more than they are exclusive of one another. In part, they exist in and through the very last poems she wrote. But, as poems written in time, by a woman aware of time, they tend to build toward that point where the second movement, a state beyond human love, can be claimed, or at least volitionally prophesied:

> There is the moon in the high window. It is over.
> (*Three Women, WT,* 55)

> We have come so far, it is over.
> ("Edge," *A,* 84)

> Once one has seen God, what is the remedy?
> Once one has been seized up
>
> Without a part left over,
> Not a toe, not a finger, and used,
> Used utterly, in the sun's conflagrations, the stains
> That lengthen from ancient cathedrals
> What is the remedy?
> ("Mystic," *WT,* 4)

Sometimes Plath depended upon the fierce repetitions of "would" or "shall" or "let us" in order to move toward and create that state beyond love. The syntax of poems like "A Birthday Present" and "Lady Lazarus" depend greatly upon such a volitional strategy. And sometimes she lent credibility to the movement she desired by indicating how far she had yet to go:

It is almost over
I am in control.

("Stings," A, 62)

Soon, soon the flesh
The grave cave ate will be
At home on me

And I a smiling woman.

("Lady Lazarus," A, 6)

The black humor of "grave cave" reappears in the phrase,
"the deep gravity of it" from another poem of hers, "A Birthday Present." In this second poem, she was also moving
away from human speech and from love.

She also wrote poems where she imagined her death at
some time in the future, which would allow for a longer
if not exactly ripe old age:

In twenty years I shall be retrograde
As these drafty ephemerids.

("Candles," CTW, 42)

But even "Candles" contains enough of the impatient
breathlessness which defined her work while in that work
she came to see life and love as increasingly impossible.

No one was more aware than Plath of what moving away
from human love in her art implied. Some important part
of her had transcended the need for the loving milk of
human kindness, or for "tenderness," as she also called it.
She set down in her poem "Mystic" a saintly impatience
with and indifference to the things of this world. And she
joined that impatience to a need and a wish to replace tenderness with some greater love:

Is there no great love, only tenderness?

(WT, 5)

Yet paradoxically, the conclusion of the poem shows the

poet unable to give up the hope she thought to renounce:

> The sun blooms, it is a geranium.
> The heart has not stopped.

(5)

In the end, then, "Mystic" contains within it a countermovement toward a belief in earthly love.

The contradictory impression which "Mystic" succeeds in conveying not only is central to the meaning of that poem, but it also connects with a defining center in much of Plath's late verse. On the one hand, there is the woman who becomes a contemporary doubting Thomas, except that what she disbelieves are not Christ's wounds and resurrected presence but his love:

> How I would like to believe in tenderness.
> ("The Moon and the Yew Tree," A, 41)

This moment is as desperate as any in modern poetry. It is as pathetic as Prufrock's musing on the mermaids, "I do not think that they will sing to me."

On the other hand, in these late poems there is an eschatology, a strategy for dying. But it is a strategy based more upon the confusions and delusions of the decadent artist than upon the calm assurance of the saint. In the drama of her *Ariel* bee poems, for example, she makes the bad joke (and double pun) of admitting that she is "boxed in." What the life-and-death drama of bees held out to her as wish and as fact was the eventual elimination of the males (cf. "It is these men I mind," from *Three Women, WT,* 50) and the survival of the queen bee through another winter and into another year. But the queen bees do not always or necessarily survive. Some die. And the bee poems indicate how stop-gap an affair the art and act of a woman-poet, beekeeper-queen bee finally are. Survival proves only temporary; and the bridal, a funeral or black Mass.

Marriage imagery is resplendent in Sylvia Plath's poetry. "Do" is recurrent and hypnotic as a word and as an action. At times the persona saying, "I do, I do," is a mechanical

doll or a prisoner confessing to a crime. These senses of
the word and phrase Plath commonly linked with the recital
of the marriage vow. "Do" also is punned upon, especially
in her poem, "Daddy." The German, familiar "du" or you
("do," "du," "you" — they even rhyme) of intimate address
and love songs is recalled, almost as a reminder of the historical and personal perversions to which love and action
can be subjected.

What Plath is "married" to obsessively occupies her in
the poems. In the larger, metaphysical sense, it is enormity
and suffering. Often, as in looking at blood-red poppies,
she feared she could not join herself to enough pain:

If my mouth could marry a hurt like that!

("Poppies in July," A, 81)

She sometimes wished and was able to transform loving
relationships between or among things and people into moments of visionary glory. But in important poems like
"Tulips," "Daddy," "In Plaster," "Mirror," "Face Lift,"
"Death & Co.," and "The Applicant," marriages or unions
prove to be inversions of love and, at their most extreme,
sadomasochistic fantasies.

The Colossus already revealed the poet's predilection for
decadent unions between love and death, and art and life.
If her browned gardenia and ghastly orchid recall fin de
siècle botanical catalogues, it is in her taste in sounds,
colors, jewels, music, painting, and literature that she shows
herself to be a contemporary decadent. Robert Lowell's attraction to the personages of Nero and Caligula and Anne
Sexton's to the distortions of Kafka and Van Gogh are out-
done by Plath — in her espousal of Brueghel, Swift, and
Leonard Baskin, in her choice of a snake for a medallion,
in her method of "deranging by harmony," and in her taste
for the absolute blankness of black and white or for sheer,
primary red. And the contents of her boudoir table and city
of mending, while going back to the catalogues of Swift
and Ovid, rival any late nineteenth-century, decadent mé-

lange.'[18] In the poems that came after *The Colossus,* however, we are able to see how this incipient decadence is turned from something faintly literary into something closer to the poet's very self: "Pom! Pom! They would have killed *me!*"

When, in *The Colossus,* Sylvia Plath felt "deadlocked" or "shut out," these feelings were often attached to very formal poems with adequate frame to allow for distance and perspective on a reader's part, as when even in seemingly deadlocked poems she concluded there was often enough ambiguity for possible survival, enough ambiguity for love and life as well as for death:

> The sun rises under the pillar of your tongue.
> My hours are married to shadow.
> No longer do I listen for the scrape of a keel
> On the blank stones of the landing.
>
> ("The Colossus," TC, 21)

> I would get from these dry-papped stones
> The milk your love instilled in them.
> The black ducks dive.
> And though your graciousness might stream,
> And I contrive,
> Grandmother, stones are nothing of home
> To that spumiest dove.
> Against both bar and tower the black sea runs.
>
> ("Point Shirley," TC, 25-26)

> Your shelled bed I remember.
> Father, this thick air is murderous.
> I would breathe water.
>
> ("Full Fathom Five," TC, 48)

> Father, bridegroom, in this Easter egg
> Under the coronal of sugar roses

---

18. My points and examples in this paragraph and some of my later arguments about decadent confusions and delusions, I discussed in my article, "Sylvia Plath and the New Decadence," *Chicago Review,* 20, No. 1 (1968), 71-73.

The queen bee marries the winter of your year.

("The Beekeeper's Daughter," TC, 74)

The concluding lines in these poems are all sufficiently open-ended to avoid tragic closure. Art and its images have not yet become the coffin or sarcophagus they would later become for her.

Considerations of art as an inheritance fascinated Plath as she wondered whether it would preserve or kill. At times, she saw art as an inheritance of revenge. Some dark biography — the rival woman, the fatherless children, the inheritance after the mother is gone — is being intently worked out in the poems. The poems now published in *Crossing the Water* and *Winter Trees* make this prominent, although the *Ariel* poems contained the same motifs. But let us leave biography and return to what the poems record.

That Sylvia Plath wrote two last-words poems, one called just that ("Last Words") and another, "Words," I find significant. The major problem which I address in this chapter — to whom and to what do her poems finally belong — the two poems engage, although in the body of her poetry they are not unique in that concern.

The poem "Words" I have already discussed, particularly in connection with my reading of the final lines as recording the image of Narcissus staring into the pool, mistaking wordless stasis for fixed stars.

"Last Words" is a very different kind of poem, closer in style to poems of intense desire like "Tulips," "A Birthday Present," or "The Arrival of the Bee Box." The poet in "Last Words" wants and volitionally unlooses herself from domestic things in order to achieve a state of utter mystic peace:

It will be dark,
And the shine of these small things sweeter than the face
of Ishtar.

(CTW, 40)

Ishtar, Babylonian and Assyrian goddess of love and fertility, is invoked. But it is the artful, statuary face of Ishtar which has importance for her in this poem. The state yearned for is death, not love. The word "sweeter" in this quotation goes back to a line earlier in the same poem, "I should sugar and preserve my days like fruit!" Sweetness commonly threatened loving deception for Plath. Here it carries equally dark connotations of preservation, but always at the unnatural expense of life. Sweetness proves costly, proves to be death.

As "Last Words" earns its authority, there emerges that tone, or "décor" — an important word for both Lowell and Plath — which related to the matter of control and to whatever triumph or failure these final poems contain.

"Last Words" manages to indicate how the poet willed to move herself and her poetry toward love as much as it indicates how she could not handle the artful business she went about. "I can't stop it," she wrote in this poem. Here "it" meant not love or blood-hurt but the escape of spirit-breath or the release of images. "Metaphors," an early poem, had talked of boarding "the train there's no getting off." Some same sense of the potential deadliness of image-making recurs in "Last Words," but in less playful terms. And it recurs in lines from other late work which includes the punning poem, "Kindness":

> The blood jet is poetry,
> There is no stopping it.
>
> (A, 82)

"Kindness" also, as I argued earlier, witnessed the poet unable to distinguish between children and roses, the intimate images she moved among. And, just as "Last Words" imagined how "they will store my heart / Under my feet in a neat parcel," so "Kindness" found loving kindness too good to be believed. Obsessively, the poet never deserted the major themes of loving, although in the very act of charting some progress or journey in which a loving context finally had been left behind.

"Last Words," like any of the major poems from *Ariel* or *Crossing the Water* or *Winter Trees*, does not dispose of the nagging sense that, in love as it may be with "a solider repose than death's" (a phrase from an early poem, "The Sculptor"), in the end, it belongs to an art of elegy, less by choice than by some desperate, pathetic necessity.

In some of her late poems, Plath was able to employ a coy perspective which still retained irony as a saving grace:

> You smile.
> No, it is not fatal.
>
> ("The Other," WT, 22)

> I do not think you credit me with this discretion.
>
> ("A Birthday Present," A, 43)

This discretion, perhaps the upper limit of the imagistic concretion she pursued in her work, gives way in too many of her other late poems to an art which has deserted lyric and love. Beginning as an art of gradations, the verse concluded by finding love unbelievable and impossible, and finally absent:

> Is this love then, this red material
> Issuing from the steel needle that flies so blindingly?
> It will make little dresses and coats,
>
> It will cover a dynasty.
> How her body opens and shuts —
> A Swiss watch, jewelled in the hinges!
>
> ("An Appearance," WT, 10)

The diminutives ("little dresses and coats") cannot conceal the fact that the material of love, however punned on, is really an art of elegy. The metaphor of art as coffin wins out and dominates all.

If the late poems belong to anyone, they belong not to her father or husband or children or even to poetry (the

sense of the poem as unloving love-child she never forgot).
But to Death, Death the lover, Death the double:

[Writing of the one]
I am not his yet.
[And of the second of the pair]
He wants to be loved.

("Death & Co.," A, 28)

She would rather be dead than fat,
Dead and perfect, like Nerfertit,

Hearing the fierce mask magnify
The silver limbo of each eye

Where the child can never swim,
Where there is only him, and him.[19]

Other poets have wooed death before or considered themselves wooed by it, among them another woman poet named
Emily Dickinson. Yet Emily Dickinson never abandoned her
wit to unloving silence but to one more ironic twist in one
more poem in the face of death.

The speculations of A. Alvarez about Sylvia Plath's death
— that it was an accident, that she hoped to be found in
time but was not — do not properly concern me here.[20]
What does concern me is the biographical weight which
poems now included in Crossing the Water and Winter
Trees add to so many of the Ariel poems, as well as the
arguments and contradictions and confusions which the
poems themselves record.[21]

---

19. Sylvia Plath, "The Fearful," The Observer, 17 February 1963, p. 23.

20. A. Alvarez, "Prologue: Sylvia Plath," The Savage God: A Study in Suicide (London: Weidenfeld and Nicolson, 1971), pp. 28-33.

21. For further support of this argument, see the poems included in the privately printed, limited editions: Sylvia Plath, Crystal Gazer and Other Poems (London: Rainbow Press, 1971); Sylvia Plath, Lyonnesse (London: Rainbow Press, 1971).

What I have been tracing — the attempts of the poems to establish lyric and love and the countermovement toward elegy and to a deadly journey which could not be stopped — gain authority and intensity from the more recently released volumes. They never contradict but extend what the *Ariel* poems were about. The old faults prove to be the same; "love cannot come here," we again find.

The moving center of both books, *Crossing the Water* and *Winter Trees,* is that of a woman of sorrows. Recurrently, Plath imagined herself as Mary and Christ. Ease, love, correspondence, and relationship all were yearned for and did not emerge. She was amazed at her continuing existence as much as she looked ahead to and made plans for a time when she would be dead and her children even more "fatherless" than she considered them then.

If some important part of Sylvia Plath in her late poetry refused to accept a world of gigolos as the final version of the world, she never abandoned the doubt that she could recognize or accept love even were she able to manage it in her life and art. As a result, tone figures more and more prominently in the interpretation of the poems she left behind. Tone, its readiness and surety, dominates.

The posthumous poems expose discrepancies and failures of the most serious kind. The phoenix figure, prominent in various guises in her work, deserted her outside her poems. And the children-poems she imagined in the late poem, "Edge," folded back into her and taken out of this life, became painfully distinct from her in death — the two children fathered by Ted Hughes and left behind; the poems which were posthumous. And the Medea figure, once little more than a literary trapping in her early poem, "Aftermath," proved in the late poem, "Edge," only a pathetic wish denied to her outside of mythology. When she died, so did her long sought-after and invoked gods.

The confusions and delusions of art and life, wish fulfillment and reality, became exposed at her death. And they record a sad fact. But, beyond that and more important, they reach back to some sense of lovelessness or lack implicit in a major part of her poetry. The *Ariel* poems, looked at together with the poems from *Crossing the Water* and *Winter Trees,* now strike me as less in love's behalf than she would have liked them to be. Poems like "Daddy" and "Lady Lazarus" in the end may not be the triumphs which their momentum and inventiveness at times celebrate. Instead, and this is my sense of them, they belong more to elegy and to death, to the woman whose "loving associations" abandoned her as she sought to create images for them. To ask us to see her as "a nude chicken neck," exposed and begging for love, is one thing. But that she was increasingly unable to write out of a tenderness for existence may be the point at which she called into question the loving movement and meanings her poems would announce. If she tried to use her poetry as a strategy for existence, the tone of the poems keeps belying that fact. Even without her suicide, too many of the late poems show the abandonment of human feeling and saving irony for a ghostlier art. In the end, her choice of metaphor for the world and for herself forced her to renounce love for a situation in which she was "roped in at the end by the one / Death with its many sticks." Death proved necessity rather than freedom and love not the season she would have liked to claim as her emblematic own.

Afterword

"Naw, Crane couldn't have ever lived," the boy said. "But he could have lived," Ginsberg cut in. "If some- body had only grabbed his cock — if he'd had enough boy friends or girl friends or whatever it was he liked."
—Allen Ginsberg in America

What these four poets evidence — two of them suicides and two of them still alive — I saw as related to the transformation of lyric and love into something of a very different order. In each chapter, I pointed to the ways in which the location of words, love, and self commonly failed. Some of that confusion related to an inability to distinguish life from art, love from fame, or loving lyric from loveless verse. If, as Galway Kinnell has written, "the dream/of all poems and the text/of all loves"[1] is that poem titled " 'Tenderness toward Existence,' " Lowell, Berryman, Cree- ley, and Plath commonly showed the achievement of or movement toward a very different art.

In the case of Lowell, we witnessed a major poet descend- ing to the desperation of writing love sonnet after love sonnet in order to get right that love and love poem which

---

1. Galway Kinnell, "Dear Stranger Extant in Memory by the Blue Juniata," *The Book of Nightmares* (Boston: Houghton Mifflin Company, 1971), p. 29.

each book sought to assert. In the case of Berryman, we witnessed another major poet struggling with the horror of love and unlove until he gave up on life in his art even before he gave up on art itself. And in the end, he gave up life and art in a suicide which, at least in one interpretation, renounced grace and love of another kind. In the case of Plath, we witnessed a brilliant young poet also giving up on life and art, doubting early whether she could ever find loving metaphors or could ever believe love or tenderness or kindness in any guise. In the case of Creeley, we witnessed a poet supposedly writing out of, in behalf of, and toward love and ease in the very act of revealing feelings and possibilities that made love and love poem not come true.

In a memoir of Berryman, William Heyen, a young poet and critic, writes:

> His marriage is what he had to have it, a storm, he said. He kept telling me that he had one very fine piece of advice for me: to focus on my wife, write about her, but to see her from someone else's perspective, his, perhaps. This was the key. Wms. must have been much the same in both ways: incredible physical stamina and need to talk and write, living the 24 hr. day; to focus on his wife through 3 novels and many poems culminating in "Of Asphodel."

Although the section on W. C. Williams could just as easily be passing through Heyen's as through Berryman's mind, what is important concerns what Berryman urged Heyen to do more than once — to write and lose himself in his wife, with love as "the only way out of the lonely reaches of the ego." If Berryman succeeded in doing this with Anne Bradstreet, he never succeeded in carrying the image of Kate, his third wife (or his daughter, Martha, for that matter) in any major way throughout The Dream Songs and the poems in the volumes that followed. And he was unable to do that, even more markedly, with the image of Christ or the Mother of God in the late religious poems. Lowell's Elizabeth Hardwick, who, along with his daughter Harriet, helped him to write the major poems of *Life Studies* and *For the Union Dead,* was replaced by a new woman-wife-dolphin who never inspired him to write great poetry. Creeley, whose wife importantly figured in and behind all of the strongest poems in *For Love, Words,* and *Pieces,* seems less in evidence as a staying image in *A Day Book* than in any of the earlier books. And Plath, perhaps a poet who lived and wrote almost before what might have been her time, found no way out of the impasse of conflicting vertical and horizontal worlds, no way toward the androgynous vision and poetry of someone like Adrienne Rich, who can be mermaid and merman, who can even cease to feel the need to write the word or concept "love" at all.

Although I have limited my considerations in this book to four poets, I would not want to dismiss them without seeing their confusions and delusions, successes and failures, major poems and failed poems, as part of that larger concern in modern poetry with what lyric can and cannot do, where love can and cannot go. In earlier referring briefly to Rich, I suggested one corner of that larger lyric background and situation. From the "big queer lonely lyrics" of Allen Ginsberg to the "short rich hard" lyrics of A. R. Ammons, from the lyric sequences of Lowell and Berryman to the Gem Tactics of Creeley and Plath, the modern American lyric continues to seek that "amateur" (amator) reader who is ideally there and waiting. My fears for some forms the lyric has taken I have expressed throughout this book. The delusions and confusions exposed by me in these poets extend from their viewing image-making as a procedure that is stop-gap or "last resort" to their mistaking "versing" and "loving" for identical habits of mind and heart. If poems are metaphoric offspring, they are not living, historical children of flesh and blood. If there is a close affinity between love and language, poets like Plath and Berryman sometimes forget that they are not the same. Language alone cannot bring love into being or make it whole. In fact, as we have seen, language continually threatens to obliterate the self, to abandon love for death. But failure is not the entire tale recorded here. I have also acknowledged, admired, and been grateful for those major lyric poems which assume and become for us primary ground: "every little word hooked to every little word, and act to act."

INDEX